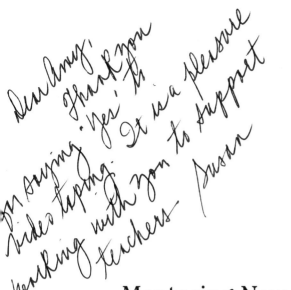

Mentoring New Teachers
Through Collaborative Coaching:
Linking Teacher and Student Learning

Kathy Dunne
Susan Villani

WestEd

ISBN: 978-0-914409-30-4

Library of Congress Control Number: 2006922980

This book is printed on 100% recycled paper.

WestEd, a national nonpartisan, nonprofit research, development, and service agency, works with education and other communities to promote excellence, achieve equity, and improve learning for children, youth, and adults. WestEd has 16 offices nationwide, from Washington and Boston to Arizona and California. Its corporate headquarters are in San Francisco.

WestEd books and products are available throughout many bookstores. To contact WestEd directly, call our Publications Center at 888-293-7833.

For more information about WestEd:

Visit www.WestEd.org

Call 415-565-3000 or toll free 877-4-WestEd

Write WestEd
730 Harrison Street
San Francisco, CA 94107-1242

Contents

Figures

Preface

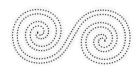

This book and its companion, *Mentoring New Teachers Through Collaborative Coaching: Facilitation and Training Guide*, are based on an earlier WestEd publication, *Mentoring: A Resource and Training Guide for Educators*. In the early stages of writing this book, we met with several of the original authors to reexamine their fundamental assumptions and beliefs about mentoring and teacher induction. The result was an affirmation and a refinement of the set of assumptions and beliefs that were articulated in the earlier publication.

Distinctive, however, in this current book and the companion facilitator's guide is the focus on collaborative coaching. Over the past decade and more, we have worked with schools and districts across the country to implement programs of professional development that incorporate a collaborative coaching model. We have also continued our long history of working in the field of mentoring new teachers. What we have found, over and over, is the importance to any mentoring program of an ongoing collaborative coaching approach — an approach in which new teachers and mentors alike reflect upon and enhance their teaching.

Basic Assumptions, Beliefs, and Goals

The information and suggestions that comprise this book are consonant with the following basic assumptions and beliefs:

- The growth and development of children is vitally linked to the growth and development of adults in and beyond schools.

- A successful mentoring program can help teachers respond intentionally with effective strategies to the needs of a diverse population of learners.

- The early years of teaching are a critical part of a continuum of learning — a link between preservice preparation and ongoing professional development.

- Mentoring is the most crucial component of the induction of new teachers in transforming the practice of teaching and is the shrewdest investment in teacher quality.
- Mentoring is part of a comprehensive plan for professional growth, grounded in what we know about adult learning and development.
- Mentoring is a demonstration of caring for individuals and the profession.
- The changing nature of schooling will continue to impact the role of the teacher and the structure of mentoring.

Building on these assumptions and beliefs, we propose three fundamental goals for effective mentor programs. The first goal is to help both new and experienced educators develop as reflective practitioners who grow by questioning their own practice. The second goal is to integrate a mentor program into the fabric of a school community by involving everyone who wishes to participate in a collaborative venture to support new teachers in ways that are mutually beneficial. And the third goal is to promote the establishment of a collegial partnership between schools and teacher preparation institutions to provide continuous professional development for educators.

Key Features of Mentor Programs

In order to achieve these goals, we propose that effective mentor programs are designed to have the following characteristics:

- responsive to the developmental needs of those whom they serve;
- grounded in the research on teacher and adult development;
- primarily supportive in nature and not linked to a formal personnel evaluation process;
- centered on enhancing knowledge and skills of new teachers in the areas of curriculum, instruction, and assessment;
- designed to provide mentors with opportunities to serve as collegial guide, seasoned teacher, consultant, and coach;
- focused on enhancing collegial connections — between mentors and new teachers, among all members of a school community, and between teacher preparation programs and schools; and
- designed as learning systems that are examined and refined to improve how they function and to add to the collaborative culture of school communities.

A common thread through these sets of assumptions, beliefs, goals, and features of mentor programs is a focus on reflective practice. When mentor and induction programs are grounded in content-based conversations about teaching and learning and are aligned with other professional development initiatives, such programs are most likely to positively impact teacher retention, teacher renewal, teacher quality, and, most importantly, student learning and achievement (Joyce & Showers, 2002).

Overview of This Resource

The primary audiences for this book include professional developers, teacher leaders, mentor and/or teacher induction program coordinators, building- and district-level administrators, and faculty from institutions of higher education. Years of research and work in the area of mentor and/or induction program design and implementation and mentor and new teacher professional development are reflected in the contents of this book. We hope that it will serve to inform the design and implementation of mentor and/or induction programs, mentor professional development, and comprehensive approaches to district-based professional development in which mentoring and induction serve as a cornerstone.

The chapters in this book are interrelated and provide an overview of key issues, research, and wisdom of practice:

Chapter 1: A Mentor Program Focused on Student Learning

Chapter 2: The Mentor Role

Chapter 3: The New Teacher's First Year

Chapter 4: Preparing Mentor Teachers as Collaborative Coaches

Chapter 1 is directed primarily to mentor program planners and directors, lead mentors, and administrators. Chapters 2, 3, and 4 speak primarily to mentor teachers and those who design and provide professional development for mentor teachers. Familiarity with the entire book will assist program facilitators to communicate with all those involved, at any level, and to anticipate and respond to the questions others may have.

The companion text, *Mentoring New Teachers Through Collaborative Coaching: Facilitation and Training Guide*, provides activities, agendas for multi-day trainings, and other resources to guide facilitators in designing and implementing effective mentor professional development.

Specifically, the facilitator's guide includes the following:

- activities to support the development and implementation of mentor-based teacher induction programs through professional development and training for mentors, new teachers, lead mentors, administrators, and other non-mentor colleagues;
- facilitator notes and step-by-step guide for implementing each activity;
- handouts, additional readings, and PowerPoint presentations to support the activities;
- references and resources that have informed the development of the guide; and
- a CD with electronic versions of the handouts and PowerPoint slides.

While we provide specific suggestions in this book and the facilitator's guide, we do so in the spirit of extending our experience, energy, and hopes rather than offering a prescription for how this work should be done. We dedicate this book to all of those who have generously shared their collective wisdom and who provide a timeless foundation for the work ahead — to mentor and coach the newest among us and continue to learn from the process.

Acknowledgements

Our journey has been guided by so many of those who have gone before us. As a result, we have been able to see differently and conceptualize anew.

We are ever grateful to authors of the original text upon which this work is based: Anne Newton, Ken Bergstrom, Nancy Brennan, Carol Gilbert, Nancy Ibarguen, Marla Perez-Selles, and Elizabeth Thomas. Their forward thinking and deep understanding of mentoring and induction of new teachers is evergreen.

Several others have offered insightful and informative reviews of this text — namely, Nancy Brennan, Charlotte Danielson, Rose Feinberg, Deborah Ireland, Melissa Lewis, and Susan Mundry. Thank you for your review, critique, and substantive influence on our final product.

We acknowledge the many endorsements of our work and send our gratitude to Nancy Brennan, Dan Conley, Charlotte Danielson, Cara Elmore, Robert Garmston, Rea Goklish, Steve Kossakoski, Elaine Pinckney, and Dennis Sparks. We are so appreciative of your generosity of intellect and spirit.

Concepts shift to reality when there are high expectations, consistent leadership, and guidance. We extend deep gratitude to Jan Phlegar for her unrelenting support and belief that this product would become a reality. Thank you, Jan.

The core content of our work is first and foremost informed by the mentors, lead mentors, new teachers, teacher leaders, school and district administrators, and state education personnel with whom we have worked. We are forever grateful to all of you.

Thank you, Kathleen Gadsby, for all of your research, securing of permissions, and ongoing disposition of "Sure, I can do that." Your consistent support behind the scenes has contributed to the quality of our work and our ability to get it done. Thank you, Kathleen.

Finally, this resource has become a reality because of the expertise, commitment, and gracious spirit of the WestEd communications team — Freddie Baer, Christian Holden, Max McConkey, Lynn Murphy, and Noel White. You have been amazing source of support and our "Rosetta Stone." Thank you all.

5

chapter ONE

A Mentor Program Focused on Student Learning

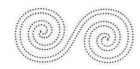

In this book, when we refer to effective mentor programs, we have a particular approach in mind — a model in which collaborative coaching plays a central role and looks at new teachers' learning as a risk-taking venture that deserves support, not judgment. As part of their induction, new teachers can benefit from collaboration with experienced mentors who will listen, observe and gather data about the teachers' effects on student learning, and facilitate their ability to understand and apply the data for their own growth and the benefit of students. Mentor programs that do less than this miss an important opportunity to increase the professionalism of all teachers in a school.

The Case for Mentor Programs

New teachers need and deserve high-quality, on-the-job support to be successful. Consider what they face. Most new teachers are expected to perform at the same level during their first years of teaching as teachers with many years of experience. Whole classrooms of students depend on new teachers from their very first days together. In addition, new teachers are likely to receive more challenging classroom assignments — and sometimes more preparations — than teachers with far more experience (Gordon & Maxey, 2000). By contrast, newcomers in many other professions have reduced responsibility coupled with significant support and supervision during their beginning years.

In the absence of this kind of support, it is not surprising that 30 to 50 percent of new teachers leave the profession within their first five years. This is not a new statistic; it has been the case for the past few decades (National Center for Education Statistics, 2001). Why is it that we continue to see such high rates of teacher attrition, despite research about interventions that improve teacher retention and years of craft wisdom about what it takes to successfully induct new teachers? A combination of old conditions that have not been addressed and new demographic and workplace realities may explain this disheartening rate of teacher attrition.

Research and experience tell us, for example, that new teachers continue to experience isolation and lack of collegiality (Ingersoll, 2001). Even when new teachers have access to mentoring and induction programs, these programs often ignore critical elements for success — those that focus on professionalism, that incorporate mentoring and induction into a continuum of career-long professional development, that promote collaboration, and that are rigorously monitored (Wong, Britton, & Ganzer, 2005; Miller, in press; Smith & Ingersoll, 2004).

Variability in how teachers are prepared leads to another cluster of challenges for new teachers. They may find themselves unprepared to respond effectively to the complex needs of increasingly diverse student populations (Bolich, 2001; Public Agenda, 2000). More teachers than ever are not prepared in the discipline that they are hired to teach, especially in mathematics and science; and increasing numbers of teachers are prepared through alternative certification pathways, which vary drastically in length and quality (Darling-Hammond, 2000).

Whatever the cause, high rates of teacher attrition result in problems for students and for the school community. In some districts, students may have inexperienced teachers for several consecutive years, sometimes even a string of inexperienced teachers during a single year. Because student achievement is linked to teacher effectiveness (Peske & Haycock, 2006; Darling-Hammond, 2000), and because new teachers are rarely as effective as experienced teachers, the more that students are taught by new teachers, the greater the challenges for ensuring high levels of learning and achievement for all students.

For the school community more broadly, failure to retain new teachers creates hardships for administrators, the other teachers, and parents. Administrators spend a great deal of time and money recruiting, orienting, and training new teachers, knowing that up to one-half of them will later leave. The coming and going of so many new teachers can take its toll on the teachers who remain. Some of the faculty may devote much time and energy to supporting new colleagues, only to see them leave within a few years of arriving. Even more disruptive, when so many faculty members are transient, it is difficult to build trust and develop a professional learning community. Parents also depend on a stable faculty in developing positive relationships with a school.

The good news is that high-quality mentor programs, as part of a comprehensive teacher induction approach, can reduce teacher attrition and improve teacher quality. Mentor programs have been able to achieve teacher retention rates of up to 90 percent — at schools that previously lost half of their new teachers — sometimes within the first year of the program (Wong, 2004; Villani, 2002). Because feelings of professional competence are crucial to new teachers' job satisfaction, mentor and induction programs that help new teachers develop knowledge and skills grounded in research and best practice can keep them in the profession. The results go beyond higher retention rates: Better supported new teachers become more effective teachers (Darling-Hammond, 2000). Well-designed mentor programs that include a significant coaching component and are allocated sufficient financial and human resources have the potential to raise student achievement (Joyce & Showers, 2002) and the teaching performance and retention of new and experienced teachers alike (Danielson, in press; Villani, 2002). (Appendix A identifies a number of historically strong mentor programs.)

More and more states are mandating mentor programs for new teachers as one way to induct them into teaching, improve their skills, and encourage them to embrace teaching as a career. In 2004, 31 states had induction programs for new teachers; 20 of those required induction for new teachers to move to different levels of certification, and 18 were supported through some level of state funding (Cavell, Blank, Toye, & Williams, 2005).

The cost of mentor programs sometimes dissuades district leaders from making mentoring a part of the induction of new teachers. Yet the financial investment required to implement a mentor program is a fraction of the financial and human resources expended because of low teacher retention. Some estimates of the associated costs of teacher turnover are 50 to 200 percent of the departing employee's salary (Texas Center for Educational Research, 2000; Norton, 1999). Proactively supporting new teachers may actually save money, in addition to all of its other benefits.

The Goals of a Mentor Program

Effective mentor programs build on new teachers' previous preparation and experiences while fostering deeper levels of instructional expertise. The goals of such mentor programs include — for both new and experienced teachers — engagement in a diverse school community, pedagogical expertise, deep content knowledge, and longevity in the profession. As culled from the literature about effective mentor programs (Odell & Huling, 2000; Fideler & Haselkorn, 1999; Shea, 1992), such programs are designed with the following purposes:

- integrate new teachers into the social system of the school, the district, and the community;

- provide practical strategies to support new teachers in effectively meeting the challenges they commonly face when entering the profession (for example, discipline, classroom management, interaction with parents, diversity in students, instructional issues);

- ensure that new teachers deepen and broaden knowledge of their content and how to teach that content;

- develop in new teachers the knowledge, skills, attitudes, and values that are vital to success throughout their careers;

- instill norms of collegiality and experimentation;

- provide instructional and interpersonal support that enhances new teachers' personal and professional development, leading to greater instructional competence;

- enhance teachers' ability and disposition to deal effectively with students, families, and colleagues who are diverse in terms of their cultural identities and learning styles;

- offer an opportunity for new and experienced teachers to analyze and reflect upon their teaching and build a foundation for the continued study of teaching; and

- retain highly qualified new and experienced teachers.

Most mentor programs are designed for teachers just beginning their careers. Some mentor programs also include teachers who are changing schools, grade levels, and/or content areas. While there are several distinctions to consider when a program includes teachers who are new to the profession *and* those who are experienced teachers but who have significantly new assignments, all teachers who are mentored with a collaborative coaching approach can benefit from the focus on student learning.

Teachers new to the profession predictably need much more support handling "survival" issues such as classroom management, dealing with parents, and cultural responsiveness. Experienced teachers with new assignments are likely to have teaching expertise that will quickly launch them over such hurdles, even in a new setting. These teachers are best served when programs recognize their past practice and help them build on it.

The Conceptual Shift from "Buddies" to Learners

Mentor programs built around a collaborative coaching approach are grounded in principles of adult learning and development and provide ongoing professional learning opportunities to mentors as well as new teachers and teachers with new assignments. Such programs can improve new teachers' and their mentors' effectiveness in the classroom. Alan Reiman and Lois Thies-Sprinthall (1998) found that the following characteristics contribute to the success of mentor programs that take a collaborative coaching approach:

- Reflection on practice is promoted through collaborative coaching and observation that is personally significant and relevant.

- Mentors, especially, receive sufficient training in collaborative coaching to capitalize on its subtleties in addition to its basic premises.

- Mentor and new teacher pairs are given sufficient time to meet and observe each other's teaching.

- The new teacher experiences a balance of supportive structures and challenging expectations.

- A mentor relationship occurs over a significant period of time — a year or more — to allow sustained interaction and recursive learning experiences.

When mentor programs include these elements, it is likely that mentors will experience a significant conceptual shift from a traditional "buddy system" that focuses on assisting new teachers with survival needs to a relational, learning-focused approach in which mentors and new teachers engage in collaborative dialogue, observation, and reflection on practice. A key for ensuring this shift is the expectation of and support for collaborative coaching grounded in classroom observations. (Appendix B outlines a yearlong program of professional development for mentors.)

Steps in Developing a Mentor Program

Whether creating a new program or revising an existing one, mentor programs require careful planning, designing, implementation, and evaluation. Typically, administrators and teachers develop a program collaboratively. It is optimal to include other members of the school community as well, such as a teachers' association member, staff developers within the school system, a member of the school board, parents, and college or university partners.

The evolution of a successful mentor program can take a number of years. Figure 1.1 presents a sample of the activities that a school can expect to undertake. As shown, ongoing evaluation and revision of various parts of a program are integral to the process.

FIGURE 1.1: SAMPLE TIMELINE FOR PLANNING, DESIGNING, IMPLEMENTING, AND EVALUATING A MENTOR PROGRAM

Task	Year 1											
	A	S	O	N	D	J	F	M	A	M	J	J
PLAN AND DESIGN PILOT PROGRAM												
School board establishes mentoring new teachers as a district priority	▓											
Multi-constituent planning group is formed or named		▓										
Planning group reviews mentoring literature, consults with experienced districts and mentoring experts			▓	▓	▓							
Planning group identifies mentor program philosophy, goals, budget; develops a proposal for school board								▓	▓			
School board considers and acts on proposal												▓
Planning group defines roles and responsibilities of participants in mentor program and criteria and procedures for selecting and assigning mentors												
Planning group conducts and analyzes preliminary assessment of needs of new teachers												
Planning group develops application form for mentors												
Planning group develops first drafts of handbooks for mentors and new teachers												
Planning group provides for the design of mentor training and the identification of professional development offered new teachers												
Planning group develops preliminary plans for evaluation and assigns staff for district follow-through												
Planning group designs plan for piloting program; determines implementation schedule and procedures												
PREPARE TO IMPLEMENT PILOT PROGRAM												
Planning group advertises for mentors, distributes application forms												
Planning group reviews applications and selects mentor pool												
Planning group collects preliminary evaluation data on the selection process; finalizes evaluation design for the pilot program												
Planning group assigns mentor/new teacher pairs; provides for scheduling of common meeting and planning time for pairs												
Planning group arranges for one-day orientation for mentors, new teachers, administrators												
IMPLEMENT AND REVISE PILOT PROGRAM												
Planning group provides for implementation of first year of pilot program; informs rest of faculty about the program; enlists their support for new teachers; publicizes program to community so families know the support new teachers will have												
Planning group revises mentor application form and selection process												
Planning group accepts applications for second cadre of mentors												
Planning group reviews applications and selects second mentor pool												
Planning group collects and analyzes evaluation data from first year of pilot program												
Planning group revises handbooks and mentoring program based on analysis of evaluation data												
Planning group assigns mentor/new teacher pairs												
Planning group provides for three- to five-day training for mentors and administrators												
Planning group provides for one-day orientation session for mentors, new teachers, administrators												

A	S	O	N	D	J	F	M	A	M	J	J	A	S	O	N	D	J	F	M	A	M	J	J

Elements of an Effective Mentor Program

Through experiences working with schools, districts, teachers' associations, state departments of education, and other education agencies, we have identified six elements of effective mentor programs:

1. Involvement of key shareholders

2. Supportive policies and procedures

3. Explicit criteria for selecting mentors and matching them with new teachers

4. Professional development and specific training for mentors

5. Administrator support and commitment

6. Mentor program evaluation

These elements can be understood in a rubric that presents them developmentally, from "emerging" through "sustainable" levels (see figure 1.2). A discussion of these elements follows. As with any rubric, this one is equally useful as a design tool or as an evaluation tool.

FIGURE 1.2: CRITERIA FOR DESIGNING AND EVALUATING MENTOR PROGRAMS

Elements of Success	Emerging	Developing	Proficient	Sustainable
Involvement of key shareholders	Mentor program is designed and planned by a few individual teachers and administrators. Could be "top down" or "bottom up."	Teachers, professionally licensed staff, and administrators work together to design the mentor program.	Teachers and administrators representing all grade levels are involved in designing and planning the mentor program.	Teachers and administrators representing all grade levels, school board members, and possibly parents and students are involved in designing and planning the mentor program. The mentor program planning team is involved in the ongoing assessment of the mentor program, identifies what's working and not working, and makes changes along the way.

Elements of Success	Emerging	Developing	Proficient	Sustainable
Supportive policies and procedures	There are no policies in place to support the mentor program, but the district has decided to implement a mentor program of some sort.	General guidelines are developed for the design and implementation of the mentor program. Incentives are provided for mentor teachers. Mentors and new teachers have to find time to meet on their own.	Specific guidelines are developed for the design and implementation of the mentor program. Incentives are provided for mentor teachers. Structures are in place to provide mentors and new teachers with time during the school day to meet and visit each other's classrooms. Lead mentors are identified within each school to coordinate logistics and serve as liaisons between administrators, mentors, and new teachers.	Specific guidelines are developed for the design and implementation of the mentor program. Incentives are provided for mentor teachers. Structures are in place to provide mentors and new teachers with time during the school day to meet and visit each other's classroom. The school schedule provides regular professional development time during the school day for all teachers, allowing new teachers to connect with and learn from other colleagues. Lead mentors are identified within each building to serve as liaisons between administrators, mentors, and new teachers; coordinate logistics; and, over a three-year period, are trained and coached to serve as mentor trainers.
Explicit criteria for selecting mentors and matching them with new teachers	No criteria exist. Building principals "handpick" mentor teachers. Mentors and new teachers are matched without consideration of grade level, content area, or geographic location. The new teacher-mentor ratio is arbitrarily decided upon and exists without necessary supports.	Mentors volunteer and are selected by a mentor program committee. No criteria exist. Mentors and new teachers are matched (to the degree possible) according to grade level and content area. The new teacher-mentor ratio is carefully considered and does not exceed a one-to-one match when mentors also have a full teaching load.	Criteria for selecting mentor teachers are identified. A mentor program committee selects mentors with input from the building principal and based upon the identified criteria. Mentors and new teachers are matched (to the degree possible) according to grade level, content area, and proximity. The new teacher-mentor ratio is carefully considered, and if it exceeds a one-to-one ratio, mentors are provided additional time to effectively support the new teachers to whom they are assigned.	Criteria for selecting mentor teachers are identified. A mentor program committee selects mentors with input from the building principal and based upon the identified criteria. Potential mentors complete an application that includes recommendations from colleagues. Mentors and new teachers are matched (to the degree possible) according to grade level, content area, and proximity. A variety of structures are provided for effectively supporting various new teacher-mentor ratios (e.g., one-to-one models, team mentoring models, grade level or content area models). A procedure exists such that, in the event matches do not work, both parties are "held harmless" and a new match is made.

Elements of Success	Emerging	Developing	Proficient	Sustainable
Professional development and specific training for mentors	Training consists of disseminating and "walking through" the new teacher handbook.	An orientation session is held for mentors to outline roles and responsibilities.

One or two days of mentor training are provided to all mentor teachers prior to the start of the school year. Training includes qualities of effective mentors, needs of new teachers, communication and questioning skills, and a demonstration of collaborative coaching.

Follow-up mentor training sessions are not provided throughout the school year. | An orientation session is held for mentors and new teachers to outline roles and responsibilities.

Three to five days of mentor training are provided to all mentor teachers prior to the start of the school year. Training includes qualities of effective mentors, needs of new teachers, active listening and questioning skills, collaborative coaching, and data gathering techniques.

Follow-up training sessions are provided throughout the school year for mentors and new teachers. | An orientation session is held for mentors and new teachers to outline roles and responsibilities.

Five days of mentor training are provided to all mentor teachers prior to the start of the school year. All building administrators attend the first day of mentor training and new teachers attend the day-five training session. Training includes qualities of effective mentors, needs of new teachers, communication and questioning skills, collaborative coaching (including opportunities for practice and feedback), data gathering techniques, and various coaching approaches.

Follow-up training sessions are provided throughout the school year for mentors and new teachers.

Mentor and new teacher pairs are provided with on-site coaching and support throughout the year, including video-based reflection on their coaching work. |
| *Administrator support and commitment* | Little or no administrator support exists beyond providing a new teacher orientation session that may or may not include mentors. | Administrators provide new teacher orientation and ensure that mentors are included, but they do not participate in other mentor program activities.

Administrators do not ensure that time is provided for mentors and new teachers to meet or observe each other. | Administrators actively support and promote the mentor program, attend mentor training sessions and administrator orientation sessions, provide mentors and new teachers with time to observe each other, and ensure that confidentiality is maintained. | Administrators actively support and promote the mentor program, attend training sessions and administrator orientation sessions, provide mentors and new teachers with time to observe each other, ensure that confidentiality is maintained, and are willing to allocate funds to sustain the mentor program (e.g., mentor stipends, release time, professional development resources and activities, mentor program evaluation activities). |

Elements of Success	Emerging	Developing	Proficient	Sustainable
Mentor program evaluation	There is no evaluation of the mentor program.	Evaluation of the mentor program focuses only on participant satisfaction with the training sessions for mentors and new teachers. A survey of new teachers' needs is conducted and used to evaluate how well the mentor program serves those needs.	Evaluation of the mentor program focuses on participant satisfaction of mentor and new teacher training sessions and assesses changes in teaching of new teachers and mentors. The impact of mentor training on supporting mentors to successfully fulfill their roles is assessed. A survey of new teachers' needs is conducted and used to evaluate how well the mentor program serves those needs. Mentor teachers self-assess their performance as mentor teachers and coaches. A rubric identifying criteria for the success of a mentor program is used to assess the efficacy of the mentor program. All of the data are analyzed and used to continually revise and improve the program.	Evaluation of the mentor program focuses on participant satisfaction of mentor and new teacher training sessions and assesses changes in teaching of new teachers and mentors. The impact of mentor training on supporting mentors to successfully fullfill their roles is assessed. A survey of new teachers' needs is conducted and used to evaluate how well the mentor program serves those needs. Mentor teachers self-assess their performance as mentor teachers and coaches. A rubric identifying criteria for the success of a mentor program is used to assess the efficacy of the mentor program. New teachers self-assess their teaching against clearly defined teaching competencies. The mentor program committee engages in an ongoing mentor program evaluation process that provides for opportunities to identify key program evaluation questions, data sources, baseline data requirements, and relevant evaluation strategies and tools. All of the data are analyzed and used to continually revise and improve the program. Data gathering and analysis include ways to assess how the program has changed teaching in ways that are likely to improve student learning and achievement.

Involvement of Key Shareholders

Key shareholders are the people who will likely shepherd the mentor program from its inception through its implementation and perhaps through the ensuing evaluation and revision of the initial program. Involving key shareholders as soon as possible — right from the planning and design stages — is crucial to the success and sustainability of a new teacher mentor program. (Appendix C is a sample of one district's elaboration of its key shareholders' roles and responsibilities.)

Administrators, faculty members (including veterans and new teachers), and other members of the school community and larger community need to view a mentor program for new teachers as a priority, especially given the fiscal pressures faced by many school districts. In addition, potential shareholders who are left out of the planning for this important work may end up sabotaging it. Consider wisely which shareholders, both specifically and as representatives of different groups, are important to invite to the table.

CONSIDER THESE QUESTIONS

➡ Who are the key people to involve, considering their influence, decision-making authority, and expertise?

➡ What other factors are important for you to consider in deciding whom to invite to participate?

➡ What role will this group of shareholders play with regard to the design and development of the mentor program? What is their level of decision-making authority?

➡ Once the mentor program is up and running, how will shareholders be involved in the ongoing evaluation of the program's effectiveness?

Supporting Policies and Procedures

A successful and self-sustaining mentor program is supported by policies and procedures that are clear to everyone and is designed to provide the time and fiscal resources necessary for the program to be carried out as intended.

Key policies, procedures, and practices address how mentors will be selected and matched with new teachers as well as how pairs can seek outside help — or even end a partnership. Time for pairs to meet, to observe, and to participate in professional development all require policies that ensure scheduled time that everyone can count on. Policies for remunerating mentors must also be specified, including, for example, how to compensate a mentor who takes on extra duties. Figure 1.3 highlights such basic policies for any mentor program.

FIGURE 1.3: BASELINE POLICIES TO SUPPORT A MENTOR PROGRAM

When planning for and designing a mentor program for new teachers, policies, procedures, and practices must at minimum address the following:

- How will mentors be selected?

- How will mentors be matched with new teachers?

- How will confidentiality be maintained?

- How will release time be provided for regularly scheduled meetings between the mentor-new teacher pairs?

- How will time be provided for mentor teachers to observe new teachers and for new teachers to observe experienced teachers?

- How will professional development be designed and scheduled for new teachers and for mentors?

- How will one or more people be chosen whose role is to confer confidentially with mentors and/or new teachers who have concerns about their partnership? A crucial assumption is that this role will not be filled by anyone who evaluates the teachers.

- How will colleagues who are not directly involved in the mentor program be involved in and/or informed about what is occurring?

- What is our "exit strategy" to provide new teachers and mentors with a no-fault process for ending their pair if the match is not a good one?

- Should we assign a "lead" mentor? What duties would a lead mentor be responsible for?

- How will mentors and lead mentors be compensated?

Scheduling the time for mentor partnerships to flourish is a challenge in most situations. Schools have come up with a number of strategies to provide release time for mentors and new teachers, ranging from creative scheduling to the use of substitutes. Figure 1.4 lists many of these suggestions.

FIGURE 1.4: STRATEGIES TO PROVIDE TIME FOR MENTOR AND NEW TEACHER PARTNERSHIPS

Schools typically combine a number of these ideas to increase the amount of time available to support participants in their mentor programs:

- Release mentors and new teachers from non-instructional duties.
- Schedule common preparation times once or twice per week for mentors and new teachers to discuss new teachers' concerns.
- Arrange for mentors and new teachers to share a common break time or lunch period for informal interaction.
- Assign mentors and new teachers to similar extra duties related to their instructional assignments.
- Employ a roving substitute one or two days each month.
- Use central office staff, building administrators, and faculty from local teacher training institutions as roving substitutes one or two times a month.
- Solicit volunteer substitute teachers, employ retired teachers, or contract with visiting teachers (for example, experts from nature centers, museums, or industry) to teach classes.
- Invite veteran teachers to present a lesson to two classes.
- Provide opportunities for team teaching, demonstration lessons, and observations that benefit students in both teachers' classrooms.

Many schools find that selecting a lead mentor is a powerful strategy. Effective lead mentors have experience in successfully serving as mentor teachers. They also have the skills and disposition to provide logistical support and coordination for the mentor program and to serve as liaisons between mentors, new teachers, and administrators. They must also be willing to be trained (over time) to take on the professional development training and facilitation needed to prepare future mentor teachers.

> What policies and procedures currently exist that would support an effective mentor program with regard to selection and matching of mentors, release time, compensation of mentors, confidentiality, etc.?

> What, if any, existing contract language would enable or inhibit implementation of the mentor program?

> What additional policies and procedures need to be established to ensure effective implementation and sustainability of the mentor program?

Explicit Criteria for Selecting and Matching Mentors With New Teachers

While it is clear that schools need policies for selecting and matching mentors with new teachers, what criteria can help ensure that these policies are effective? Through many experiences across the country, we have identified essential mentor selection criteria within five primary categories: proximity, stewardship, knowledge, skills, and dispositions.

Proximity. In addition to a mentor's physical proximity — a classroom in the same building if not right down the hall from the new teacher — "content proximity," having experience with the same or similar grade or content area as the new teacher, is extremely helpful.

Stewardship. Mentors represent their schools to new teachers, so they must have a genuinely positive outlook on their school's culture, climate, and possibilities. They also must be professionally credible. This includes having a minimum number of years of teaching experience and the high regard of their colleagues.

Knowledge. Mentors must have deep content and pedagogical knowledge, including knowledge of national, state, and local curriculum standards and of various methods of assessing student learning and achievement. Mentors must also know and be able to represent district policies and procedures to new teachers.

Skills. Beyond content-specific instruction and assessment skills, mentors must have effective listening and questioning skills and a collaborative approach in working with others. They must be able to respond respectfully and knowledgeably to those whose teaching philosophies or cultural backgrounds differ from their own.

21

Dispositions. Successful mentor teachers have a disposition to be of service to new colleagues. They are willing to share ideas, materials, resources, and strategies. They are comfortable inviting new teacher partners into their classrooms, and they are open to learning with and from new teachers. They understand and enjoy their roles as consultant, coach, colleague, and guide.

Identifying mentor selection criteria not only guides the selection of the most suitable candidates for the role, but it also spurs the people planning a mentor program to explore program values and what to focus on when designing mentor professional development.

Communicating the selection criteria publicly to mentor and non-mentor colleagues alike signals to the school community that mentoring is a significant role and requires expertise, training, and specific dispositions. It also conveys an objective selection process, which tends to increase the number of applicants and supports those making the selection decisions.

Investing time in developing selection criteria and a process for choosing mentors will help ensure that the program gets off to a good start and can save considerable time and avoid trouble later. However, it is not always possible to follow the ideal process for selecting and matching mentors and new teachers. In smaller schools and/or rural areas, for example, there may be only one position in a particular content or specialty area. In that case, it would become necessary to match a new teacher with a mentor who is teaching in a related content area or grade level. Some districts assign two mentors for a new teacher who is in a building having no other teacher of his or her content area, such as mathematics or special education. The mentor within the building can focus on school culture while the mentor specializing in the same content area (located in a different building) can be the new teacher's collaborative coaching partner.

Another factor influencing matches is the number of new teachers versus the number of mentors who have similar teaching assignments. In large schools and urban centers, for example, achieving a one-to-one ratio of mentors to new teachers may not be possible if new teachers outnumber available mentors. These circumstances require creative matching and alternative mentoring structures, such as peer coaching or mentoring teams in which one mentor teacher serves a group of new teachers. In such cases, some, if not all, of the new teachers will be teaching in different content areas or grade levels from the mentor.

- What, if any, criteria exist for selecting people to serve in other teacher leadership roles in our setting? How might these criteria inform the mentor selection criteria?

- What will the process be for selecting and matching mentors? Who will make the final decision?

- How will we ensure that the process is fair and equitable?

- How will the mentor selection criteria and process be communicated to all staff members, community members, and potential funders?

Professional Development and Specific Training for Mentors

Like new teachers, new mentors also need training and coaching to be effective in their roles. Even excellent classroom teachers may not necessarily know how to coach other adults effectively. The kind of professional development available to mentors can make the difference between a mentor program being a minimally useful "buddy system" versus its being a program that can support new teachers and enhance their effectiveness.

Investing in mentor training and professional development provides benefits that spread beyond the new teachers and across a school community. Mentor teachers, for example, often find that their own practice improves as a result of the coaching they do to help new teachers to be reflective and intentional about their practice. Experienced teachers are often re-energized by the learning and collegiality they gain through the process. Mentoring relationships of this sort can contribute to a school culture of collaboration and reflection, dramatically affecting the student and adult members of the school community.

Mentor training and other professional development support need to be well-planned and ongoing. An initial day or two of orientation to the mentor role is only a beginning. Mentors need to learn how to coach and facilitate the growth of their new teacher partners. This learning requires time, practice, and regularly scheduled professional development. We have found that an initial four- to five-day training session for mentors, followed by three to four additional professional development days throughout the school year, provides the solid foundation and timely support that mentors need to be most effective in their roles. In addition to these more formal training events, learning will occur on a daily basis as mentors and new teachers talk informally together and with other mentors, colleagues, new teachers, and administrators. Figure 1.5 lists key content to include in mentor training. Chapter 4 offers a focused exploration of the collaborative coaching aspects of mentor professional development.

FIGURE 1.5: ESSENTIAL CONTENT FOR MENTOR TRAINING

When designing professional development and specific training for mentors, essential content includes knowledge and skills for mentors to understand and apply as they model and coach new teachers:

- Research on the needs of new teachers and implications for a mentor's role
- Roles and responsibilities of mentor program participants (mentors, new teachers, administrators, non-mentor colleagues)
- General communication skills
- Collaborative coaching skills, including questioning and conferencing techniques
- Coaching observation approaches and data gathering strategies
- Framework for examining teaching, learning, and assessing

CONSIDER THESE QUESTIONS

➡ What other professional development have we tried in the past to train mentors and/or coaches in any capacity? What were the results of the training? What are some implications for the current design and implementation of mentor training?

➡ What other professional development initiatives are in place? And what, if any, relationship do they have to the professional development and training of mentors?

➡ When and how often will follow-up training for mentors take place?

Administrator Support and Commitment

Support and commitment from district and site-level administrators means that a mentor program will be adequately resourced, valued by the school community and parents, and poised for success.

Central office administrators may need to be convinced to dedicate sufficient resources to support a mentor program that goes beyond a buddy system. To recognize the importance of a mentor program modeled on collaborative coaching, they may need to more fully understand the needs of new teachers and the ways that a mentor program can affect teacher retention and quality of practice. In addition, a cost-benefit analysis comparing the expense of a mentor program versus the costs of recruitment, hiring, training, and evaluating new teachers to replace those who leave the profession prematurely can be an important piece of evidence to ensure central office commitment.

When a mentor program is in place, most administrators are supportive if they have sufficient advance notice to make the necessary preparations. Building-level administrators can do many things to support mentors and new teachers. In addition to respecting the confidentiality of the mentoring relationship, building-level administrators can support a mentor program by encouraging experienced staff members to apply to become mentors. Administrators can make sure that faculty members who currently are not in the mentor program understand the value of mentoring and how they too can assist new teachers. Principals can also make sure that new teachers are not given the most difficult teaching assignments or preparations and that their schedules allow them common planning time with their mentor partners. (Appendix D provides a checklist of various ways that principals can support a mentor program.)

Sometimes principals feel that the relationship between mentors and new teachers lessens the importance of their own relationships with new teachers or limits an aspect of their job that they most enjoy — supporting novices to discover the joys of enhancing their teaching practice. Site administrators also may feel left out because of the need for confidentiality between mentors and new teachers. But confidentiality is necessary to ensure a clear distinction between teacher supervision and the mentoring process. Administrators should not be privy to conversations between the mentor and new teacher unless, of course, there is an issue of student safety that must be addressed. Therefore, it is critical to design and describe the mentor program in ways that invite all members of the school community to support new teachers, while clearly designating specific roles and responsibilities to ensure that confidentiality is maintained.

➡ How will administrators be provided with opportunities to learn about and understand the goals of the mentor program and their roles? What will their level of participation be in mentor training sessions?

➡ What will be the role of administrators in the selection of mentors? Who else will be involved in the mentor selection process?

➡ How might administrators provide connections between the hiring process and the mentor program?

➡ How will administrators ensure that confidentiality is maintained between mentors and new teachers?

Mentor Program Evaluation

Evaluation ensures that a program evolves as needed to become most appropriate for its context. After a mentor program is designed and initiated, gathering and analyzing feedback from program participants and students will shed light on the impact of the program. Planning group members will need to decide what types of data and data gathering strategies are most appropriate in their setting and will result in the most useful information.

Program evaluation is sometimes overlooked because districts are eager to put all their resources into "direct" services for new teachers and their mentors. However, building program evaluation into the mentor program process will make it possible to efficiently collect the baseline data needed to measure the impact of a mentor program, to make improvements, and to positively influence continued funding. A powerful resource for effective mentor program evaluation is *Collaborative Evaluation Led by Local Educators* (Brackett, 2004), which can be found online at http://www.neirtec.org/evaluation. This free tool leads users step-by-step through a collaborative evaluation process.

Who needs to be involved in the mentor program evaluation process?

What are the overarching evaluation questions to be answered?

What data need to be gathered to answer the evaluation questions? What data sources already exist?

What data gathering tools and/or strategies will be used to gather additional data?

How will the results of data gathering and analysis be used?

Finally, from our own experiences and those of many colleagues across the country, we know that certain policies, procedures, and attitudes — about time, confidentiality, administrative support, compensation, and communication with other teachers at a school — can make or break even the best-intended mentor programs. Figure 1.6 lists key questions to keep a mentor program on track.

FIGURE 1.6: FIVE QUESTIONS TO KEEP ASKING

Evidence from mentor programs across the country indicates that continually asking and answering the following questions allows the designers and supporters of a mentor program to gauge how well they are meeting the key policy considerations in the success of a mentor program.

1. How is time being provided for mentors and new teachers to observe in each other's classrooms? If release time is not being provided, why not? How can this be resolved?

2. How is confidentiality between mentors and new teachers and between administrators and mentors being maintained? If confidentiality is not being maintained, why not? What needs to happen?

3. What types of administrative support for the mentor program are evident? Which support is most helpful and why? What else needs to happen?

4. If mentors are being compensated for their work, is compensation being addressed in timely ways? If not, why not? What needs to happen?

5. How are colleagues who are not directly participating in the mentor program being involved and/or informed about what is occurring? What could increase the involvement of all school staff members in the success of the mentor program?

chapter TWO

The Mentor Role

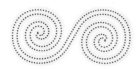

The purpose of this chapter is to make explicit the roles and responsibilities of effective mentors, identify essential elements in building trusting relationships, and examine some potential challenges in the mentor-new teacher relationship and ways of dealing with these challenges. As crucial as the mentor role is, mentoring should be seen as just one aspect of new teacher induction, integrated into a comprehensive professional development plan for new teachers' first year(s) in the classroom. (Appendix E identifies the range of topics to be included in new teacher induction.)

29

Mentor Roles and Responsibilities

Mentors' roles are complex. School systems all too often construe mentorship as little more than a "buddy system" to show new teachers the ropes and help them survive the first year of teaching. Addressing survival concerns is necessary but not sufficient. New teachers also need focused attention on developing and deepening their teaching practice to ensure learning for all students.

Effective school and district decision-makers recognize and support the multiple roles that mentors play and the value they provide. Among mentors' most important roles are those of collegial guide, seasoned teacher, consultant, and coach (see figure 2.1). These roles blend together as mentors engage in day-to-day interactions with their new teacher partners. As the new teachers' concerns shift during the year, the emphasis among the roles changes.

FIGURE 2.1: FOUR MENTORING ROLES

The mentor's role shifts during the school year, depending on the needs of the new teacher at the time, but typically it incorporates the following roles:

- Acting as a **collegial guide**, the mentor helps orient and acclimate the new teacher to the culture of the school and community and responds to the new teacher's immediate and evolving needs.

- When acting as a **consultant**, the mentor actively supports the new teacher in identifying strategies for managing and resolving struggles that arise from interactions with others, such as colleagues or parents.

- As a **seasoned teacher**, when the new teacher asks for input/insight, the mentor shares the wisdom and practical knowledge of experience. In the role of seasoned teacher, the mentor also should model professionalism, collegiality, and lifelong learning.

- In the role of **coach**, the mentor leads the new teacher through a process of collaborative inquiry that expands and improves the new teacher's instructional repertoire.

The Role of Collegial Guide

At the beginning of the year, orienting a new teacher is obviously important. This pressing need calls for the mentor to serve primarily in the role of collegial guide. A new teacher will have questions about available resources, procedures, and the school personnel and facility. A mentor can help address these concerns by providing information such as a brief outline of school personnel and their responsibilities, a suggested list of procedures to help begin each school day, a beginning-teacher calendar checklist, and a calendar of mentor activities throughout the school year.

Providing essential information is not the only way to help acclimate a new teacher to a new school. Sometimes a bit more subjective view of the situation is in order. The new setting often needs to be interpreted or clarified for a newcomer. A mentor may help answer questions about the school culture:

- How does this school really work?
- Who are the "go to" people for information, materials, resources, etc.?
- What does this school do well?
- Where does this school have problems?

- How does the history of this school account for the way it is now?

- How can a new teacher come to understand this school's culture?

In order to answer such questions honestly and openly, the mentor may have to admit biases to the newcomer and then encourage the new teacher to develop her or his own opinions.

Ultimately, mentoring is about more than introducing the new teacher to the school and its idiosyncrasies. Another aspect of being an effective mentor is modeling collegiality. In some instances, a new teacher can learn simply from watching a mentor interact effectively with others, for example, when collaborating in grade-level meetings, developing lesson plans or examining student work with peers, participating in school decision-making, and meeting with parents. At other times, the mentor models collegiality directly in the way she or he engages with the new teacher. For example, the mentor may share teaching ideas and materials, assist the new teacher in developing lessons or assessments, and help the new teacher prepare for formal evaluation with the principal or other supervisors.

Another important way for mentors to promote collegiality is by connecting new teachers to other colleagues who can become invaluable resources. By focusing on being of service to new teachers, mentors can help build collegial connections not only for new teachers, but for the entire teaching staff.

The Role of Consultant

New teachers sometimes find themselves in difficult situations with others (colleagues, administrators, staff, students, parents, or community members). In such cases, mentors serve as consultants for new teachers, helping them sort out these challenges and standing by them as they work through difficult situations. For example, a new teacher may ask a mentor to sit in as the new teacher speaks with a colleague, parent, or administrator. Being present in this way does not mean the mentor must always agree with the new teacher, but it does mean protecting the new teacher's opportunity to express a point of view. This mentor role also involves helping the new teacher advocate for herself or himself. Additionally, a mentor can sometimes advise the new teacher on how to anticipate and avoid some common pitfalls.

The politics in a school can discourage a beginner. The new teacher may need somewhere to vent frustrations without being judged. A mentor can act as a sounding board and can also look out for the new teacher in the event that inappropriate or overwhelming demands are made of the novice. A mentor may help the new teacher put political predicaments into a context that she or he can understand or may help facilitate their resolution.

The Role of Seasoned Teacher

In the role of seasoned teacher, mentors represent the professionalism developed over years of increasingly effective classroom management and instruction. New teachers can appreciate them as artful teachers with valuable experience to share.

Assistance with discipline and classroom management is the most frequently perceived need of new teachers (Moore-Johnson, & The Project on the Next Generation of Teachers, 2004; Moir, 1999; Veenman, 1984). There are many ways for mentors to address this. They may share different strategies to help new teachers get started. Mentors may tell new teachers about the way they organize their own classrooms and suggest other teachers' strategies for classroom management. In fact, mentors may invite new teachers into their classrooms to observe them; they may also suggest that new teachers observe other masterful teachers to see what policies and procedures they implement to ensure positive student behavior.

As important as it is to know different procedures and strategies for discipline and classroom management, new teachers will be significantly more effective if they also consider classroom management based on knowledge of and respect for students' different cultural norms. Understanding students' cultural identities helps new teachers create culturally responsive classroom environments, including culturally responsive units of instruction. A recent study found that when teachers are adequately prepared and supported to be culturally responsive, their students benefited in a number of ways. When participating in interactive instruction, students were found to be on task 90 percent of the time, and they demonstrated higher achievement levels on standardized assessments than peers not being taught in culturally responsive classrooms. In addition, students in culturally responsive classrooms improved their perceptions of their sense of belonging, their own ability to do well academically, and their families' expectations of them (Hughes et al., 2004).

Not everyone agrees on when to introduce new teachers to new ideas or practices. New teachers are understandably overwhelmed with all they have to do in their first year of teaching. Mentors and program directors might think issues of equity, diversity, and culturally responsive education can be put off until teachers have mastered the basics of classroom management, curriculum, and instruction. However, the first few years of teaching are when teachers formulate and refine their practices and beliefs about teaching, based on their new experiences. Without deep knowledge of diverse cultures and equity concerns, new teachers are denied some of the most powerful tools of teaching. New teachers cannot afford to wait to become more knowledgeable about these issues. They need to know all they can as they begin teaching and then continue to learn more.

There are similar debates about whether professional development for new teachers should include a content-specific focus. While there may be a tendency to defer focusing on content until classroom management and familiarity with their school's culture are established, educators increasingly are recognizing the value of and, in many cases, insisting on incorporating content knowledge and pedagogy in the training and support of new teachers. In fact, some studies suggest that if the teacher has a command of the content *and* how to teach it, their students are more engaged and classroom management issues are minimal (Nave, 2006).

The Northern New England CoMentoring Network, a four-year National Science Foundation-funded project, was designed to prepare experienced secondary mathematics and science teachers to serve as mentors to new teachers of mathematics and science at the secondary level. One of the initiative's key findings related to how two subsets of mentors balanced content, content-related pedagogy, and support around survival issues. One subset engaged in content-specific supports for new teachers at a faster rate. New teachers served by this subset of mentors reported a higher level of comfort in teaching their respective content and a greater use of content-based tools and resources in their daily planning and instruction. Additionally, these new teachers reported fewer personal and management concerns than is usually the case for new teachers.

While new teachers will have learned about pedagogical theory and curriculum in traditional preparation programs, their exposure to teaching methods may have been limited. For those new teachers entering the profession via alternative certification routes, knowledge of instructional strategies may be even sketchier, presenting an even greater need for mentoring and professional development support (Darling-Hammond, 2000).

To reiterate, mentoring support and other professional development support are complementary parts of new teacher induction and must include focusing on the mechanics of good teaching, the content being taught, and the fundamental principles and knowledge that are the foundation for promoting the growth and achievement of all students.

The Role of Coach

From the mentoring side of new teacher induction, the mentor's signature role in a collaborative coaching model is that of a coach, guiding a new teacher through reflective conversations about teaching and learning. Within this role, a mentor provides instructional leadership by talking with the new teacher about teaching, probing as the teacher plans instruction, observing the new teacher, and gathering objective data that can inform future classroom lessons. As a coach, the mentor may assist a new teacher with many of the same issues that come up in other roles, but the approach is one that carefully structures planning, observation, and reflection to promote a new teacher's personal construction of knowledge. The mentor as coach may assist in the following important areas:

- organizing and planning instruction;
- managing time and stress;
- creating a positive and reflective learning environment for students;
- learning to identify effective classroom resources (for example, curriculum materials, standards-based lessons, and rubrics and other formative assessment tools);
- learning the relevant subject-area research and standards;
- developing a repertoire of instructional strategies; and
- interacting with and relating to parents and families.

Because the coaching role is so central to being an effective mentor for new teachers, we cover coaching in more detail in Chapter 4: Preparing Mentor Teachers as Collaborative Coaches.

Regardless of which role the mentor is filling at any given time, certain approaches and values are implied. Across all roles, mentor behavior needs to be nonjudgmental, open-minded, reflective, respectful, empathetic, confidential, and realistically optimistic (Lipton & Wellman, 2001; Reiman & Thies-Sprinthall, 1998; Moir, 1999). For example, when sharing personal insights and practices, the mentor should honor the new teacher's individuality and encourage innovation and exploration. By establishing a confidential relationship, the mentor offers a context that can be safe and stimulating simultaneously. The new teacher can build confidence in his or her teaching abilities while still identifying challenges and exploring strategies to address them. Likewise, through responsible, consistent, and open-minded attitudes and behaviors, the mentor gradually establishes a trusting relationship with a new teacher that allows both of them to explore the teaching profession through a free and useful exchange of ideas.

To be effective in the various roles that mentors must assume, certain knowledge and skills come into play:

- understanding the purposes and desired results of effective mentoring;

- being able to apply norms of collaboration that promote effective communication and problem solving;

- using a coaching process that includes planning conversations, coaching observations, and reflecting conversations;

- understanding a standards-based approach to teaching and learning (e.g., National Science Education Standards, NCTE Standards for English Language Arts, and NCTM Mathematics Standards);

- using a self-assessment to measure effectiveness as a coach of a new teacher; and

- being able to prioritize the mentor role relative to other non-classroom school commitments.

Building the Relationship With a New Teacher

At the heart of mentoring is a positive, collaborative relationship between an experienced educator and a new teacher. A supportive, encouraging, trusting relationship is essential to the success of the induction experience. Such a relationship has the best chance of success when the following conditions exist:

- Clear expectations are established for the mentoring partnership.

- The mentor is skillful in understanding himself or herself and others.

- The mentor is able to assist (not assess) new teachers.

- A no-fault exit strategy is in place.

Establishing Clear Expectations

In the first meeting with a new teacher, a mentor needs to be very clear about expectations for the mentoring relationship — for example, the mentor's role and responsibilities, goals for the mentoring experience, and time restrictions. For the initial meeting, the mentor might present a draft of her or his expectations and ask the new teacher to draft a parallel set of expectations. Presenting expectations in written form is helpful for both parties; discussion of both sets of expectations becomes a focus of the mentoring relationship.

Statements of expectations should address those the partners have of each other and those that partners can expect of the administration in terms of time and other resources (see figure 2.2).

FIGURE 2.2: STATING EXPECTATIONS

It is wise to begin a new mentoring relationship with written statements from each partner about what each expects and can promise, personally and professionally. This is also the time to make scheduling commitments.

Mentor's expectations and commitment: What the mentor expects of the new teacher and what the mentor promises regarding support, assistance, and personal commitment

New teacher's expectations and commitment: What the new teacher expects of the mentor and what the new teacher promises regarding support, assistance, and personal commitment

Time and scheduling: What the administration has promised in terms of time for meeting together and other professional development and how that time will support the mentoring relationship

A first meeting between the mentor and new teacher also should include developing a preliminary plan for coaching conversations and visiting each other's classroom, starting with informal visits before the formal coaching process begins. The mentor should discuss a proposed plan of action with the principal, department head, or supervisor in advance of this first meeting in order to gain support for the expectations of the mentoring relationship. It is also important for the mentor and new teacher to meet together with the principal to share their plans and work out release time, substitute coverage, schedules, or whatever else might be needed.

Understanding Oneself and Others

The success or failure of a mentoring relationship can hinge on the levels of trust and rapport that begin to develop early in the relationship. For new teachers, trust means developing a sense of safety and openness, which is then sustained throughout the mentoring relationship. Rapport depends on all the ways in which mentors and new teachers are able to interact comfortably with one another — for example, how they share ideas, information, and challenges; how they use humor; and how they handle both the easy and the difficult issues that may arise between them.

Effective mentoring relationships are also based on the mentor's ability to be empathetic and analyze why a teacher might behave in particular ways. To be able to support the new teacher's personal and professional growth, a mentor needs to understand how adults develop, learn, react, and change. Knowing what a new teacher thinks, feels, and believes requires a continuous effort on the part of the mentor to make predictions about the new teacher's behaviors while interacting with her or him. This skill is similar to how experienced teachers assess their own classroom dynamics by simultaneously analyzing, judging, predicting, and redirecting the course of action. Mentor teachers need to draw upon this ability to provide new teachers with appropriate supports and challenges. The mentor's careful appraisal of interactions with a new teacher will impact the quality of the mentoring relationship and inform the mentor's choice of support strategies.

In addition to understanding adult development, the mentor should also know about the change process and the dynamics of diversity and their impact on people's behavior and values.

Building a strong relationship also depends on accurate self-perception. A mentor should have a predisposition to self-analysis and reflection and recognize that gaining self-knowledge is a complex process that occurs over a lifetime. For example, a mentor benefits from knowing her or his individual strengths and weaknesses, beliefs and attitudes, and preferences and prejudices, since these will likely help or hinder communication with others.

Real or perceived differences play an important role in the way people "read" others — making predictions about them and analyzing and judging them. Differences in age, gender, culture, language, race, religion, learning styles, political orientation, sexual orientation, socioeconomic status, and national origin can challenge a mentor's understanding of how to effectively communicate and build a relationship with a new teacher. When commonalities are not readily identified, the more information a mentor has about the other person — the deeper the mentor's understanding of the new teacher's perspective — the better equipped the mentor will be in providing the needed support at the right time. Additionally, it is crucial that mentors and new teachers heighten their collective awareness and understanding of the role that culture plays in their daily interactions and communication with others.

For many reasons, the levels of trust and rapport needed for an effective mentoring relationship may not evolve easily. Some of the most difficult barriers to establishing trust and rapport are differences in perceptions, values, and/or beliefs between the mentor and new teacher. In our observations, these differences are often about teaching philosophy, experiences within contrasting classroom settings, experiences with different school cultures, or even the perceived need for the mentor relationship. Additionally, when mentors and new teachers come from different cultural backgrounds, important distinctions can surface that have implications for developing trust and rapport. Another potential barrier emerges when schools require mentors to assess or evaluate new teachers versus having mentors serve in a non-evaluative role. Whatever the challenge in developing trust and rapport, what matters most is recognizing any discord, naming it, and then talking about it honestly in terms of its implications and possible resolutions.

Assisting (Not Assessing) the New Teacher

As mentioned, one of the key factors in developing trust and rapport in mentoring relationships is the decision to treat the mentor-new teacher relationship as one of assistance and support versus one in which the mentor supervises, assesses, and evaluates the new teacher. Many programs separate the roles of assistance and assessment because they believe it leads to greater levels of trust and more open and honest sharing by new teachers about challenges they face and areas where they may lack confidence (Villani, 2002). Principals, for example, sometimes find that new teachers are reluctant to be candid with them about concerns and challenges if the principal is also the teacher's evaluator. Having mentors with whom new teachers can openly share real struggles and challenges is an opportunity to better prepare new teachers for meaningful evaluation.

Some counterviews, however, hold that blending assistance and assessment can add to the rigor of support and accountability for new teachers (Feiman-Nemser, 2001). Programs that have successfully blended mentor assistance and assessment include the Rochester, New York, and the Columbus, Ohio, Peer Assistance and Review (PAR) programs (Villani, 2002). PAR programs are used to address teacher quality and retention through agreements between the teachers' union and administration. In these programs, guidelines prescribe the responsibilities of the mentors. The mentors work to maintain a balance between collegiality and supervision and evaluation, and the new teachers understand the parameters.

While this balance may be effective in certain circumstances, in our experience, programs in which the mentor's role is one of assistance rather than supervision and evaluation are often more successful at creating a professional learning community in which teachers feel free to observe colleagues and be observed, genuine conversations about teaching and learning are more likely to occur, and teachers are more apt to identify areas of needed growth.

Having an Exit Strategy

The vast majority of mentoring partnerships work well and can be improved by reflection and honest communication about the strengths and challenges of the relationship. As with any relationship, it takes work to build and keep it strong. However, once in a while, a mentoring relationship does not work for one or both of the participants. If efforts to reconcile or redefine a relationship fail to establish the necessary communication and trust, it is important to have a predefined exit strategy in place.

Ending a struggling relationship should be the solution of last resort, but the option needs to exist and carry no judgment about either the new teacher or mentor. Everyone in the program should understand the exit process. Ideally, a designated person or group of people is available to help address any concerns about the mentor program or individual partnerships. None of these people should have supervisory or evaluation responsibilities for the new teachers or mentors so that no one has to worry about the impact on evaluations of discussing a relationship that is not working and why. With a neutral colleague or group of colleagues — lead mentors or mentor program planning committee members often serve in this role — it should be possible to discuss the issues openly and in ways that help the program advisors make another, more promising mentor assignment for the new teacher. Every new teacher needs an effective mentor, and no new teacher (or mentor) should feel defeated by an initial partnership that needs to be changed.

CONSIDER THIS

If efforts to redefine or reconcile a particular mentor and new teacher relationship have not been successful, a different mentor must be assigned to the new teacher without judgment about either the new teacher or the mentor. And even with an exit strategy in place, it may be necessary to continue to support both the mentor and new teacher to ensure that they experience the change as a no-fault resolution.

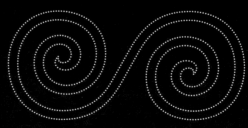

chapter THREE

The New Teacher's First Year

The needs of a new teacher are broad and complex. Over the course of the new teacher's first year, mentors will find themselves responding to a range of issues. Many of these are developmental and will change across the year. Mentors need to be familiar with what a new teacher is likely to be grappling with, as well as the likelihood that at different times of the year the new teacher's needs for information and skills will shift. This chapter introduces the predictable phases and stages that a new teacher experiences and describes how the mentor can anticipate these phases and stages to provide specific types of support when they are most needed. In addition, this support will be even more useful as the mentor develops a shared understanding of effective teaching with the new teacher.

41

Developmental Attitudes and Needs

We have found Ellen Moir's (1999) description of the phases of attitudes toward teaching and Simon Veenman's (1984) continuum of new teacher concerns to be particularly useful in preparing mentors (and new teachers) to know what to expect. Each describes predictable, developmental behaviors or feelings that most new teachers experience during their first year of teaching.

Attitudinal Phases in the First Year

Ellen Moir and colleagues at the New Teacher Center at the University of California, Santa Cruz, have identified predictable phases of a first-year teacher's attitude toward teaching. Typically, a beginning teacher's attitudes range from anticipation to survival to disillusionment to rejuvenation to reflection and back to anticipation. Figure 3.1 depicts how these phases generally occur over the course of the first year of teaching.

FIGURE 3.1: PHASES OF A FIRST-YEAR TEACHER'S ATTITUDE TOWARD TEACHING

1. **Anticipation Phase:** Before new teachers start their first assignment, they are idealistic, excited, and anxious.

2. **Survival Phase:** During the first month of school, new teachers are bombarded with a variety of problems and situations that they have not anticipated. Besides planning and preparing lessons, new teachers are responsible for organization tasks such as taking lunch counts, announcing PTA fundraising drives, and establishing classroom routines and procedures.

3. **Disillusionment Phase:** Around November, new teachers begin to question their commitment and their competence. They are faced with Back to School Night, parent conferences, and observations by their principals. Just when they are running fast to keep pace with varied obligations, they need to run even faster to keep up. It is a time of distress. Surviving this phase may be the toughest challenge for new teachers.

4. **Rejuvenation Phase:** After winter break, new teachers feel rested and rejuvenated. There is a slow rise in their attitudes. They come back with renewed hope and a better understanding of the job. They are relieved that they have survived the first half of the year.

5. **Reflection Phase:** This is the time teachers review their curriculum, classroom management, and teaching strategies. It is a "what worked and what will I do differently" stage. The end of the year is approaching, and they start thinking about the next year. It is a time of self-analysis.

6. **Anticipation "Phase II":** Having experienced their first year of teaching with its successes and challenges and the various accompanying attitudes, new teachers typically end the year with a fresh anticipation and excitement as they look ahead to their next year of teaching.

Note. From "The Stages of a Teacher's First Year," by E. Moir, 1999, in *A Better Beginning: Supporting New Teachers,* Marge Scherer (Ed.), Alexandria, VA: Association for Supervision and Curriculum Development. Copyright 1999 by Association for Supervision and Curriculum Development. Adapted with permission.

For some new teachers, the phases may not happen in exactly the way identified by Moir. For instance, some teachers speak about disillusionment happening before survival, or indicate that survival concerns are prevalent all year long. For some teachers, reflection is not a feature of a particular period but rather happens throughout the year. What is most important about Moir's phases is that they identify possibilities that mentors can anticipate — planning interactions with their new teachers accordingly. Because the sense of isolation that new teachers experience is often one of the most difficult parts of their transition into the profession, knowing that other teachers have experienced the same feelings may reduce their sense of aloneness and uncertainty. Mentors can help new teachers understand the developmental nature of their first year.

A Continuum of New Teacher Needs

In his seminal work with over a thousand beginning teachers, Simon Veenman (1984) discovered that there were predictable times during the first year of teaching when new teachers would express specific concerns and needs. Similar to Moir's description of the phases of new teachers' attitudes, figure 3.2 depicts Veenman's findings about the specific times of the year when different types of mentor support are needed most.

FIGURE 3.2: MENTOR SUPPORT ACROSS THE NEW TEACHER'S FIRST YEAR

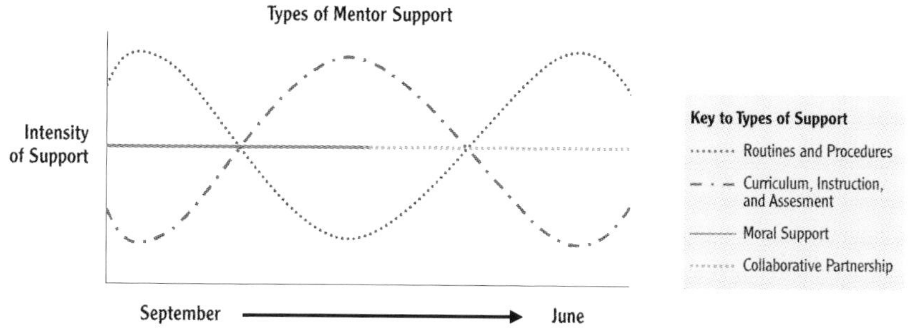

Note. Developed from "Perceived Problems of Beginning Teachers," by S. Veenman, 1984, *Review of Educational Research, 54* (2).

Not surprisingly, routines and procedures are likely to be the main topics of conversation at the beginning of the year. Topics might include how to establish classroom routines; how to communicate with the front office about attendance, a discipline problem, or a medical emergency; and where to find supplies or duplicate materials.

Typically, after the first couple of months when the policies of the school and the routines of the classroom are well-established, new teachers are more focused on concerns related to curriculum, instruction, and assessment. New teachers may want to know effective ways to teach a particular aspect of the curriculum, how to assess student learning while they are teaching, or how to design lessons that also meet the local and/or state curriculum standards. These needs and concerns remain as "front-burner" issues for the majority of the school year. During this time, mentors and new teachers focus their work together on teaching practice, using a variety of methods — for example, conversations about lesson plans, classroom observations between the mentor and new teacher, observing other teachers within the school, and examining student work and assessments.

What often surprises new teachers is the number of survival issues they also have in the spring. Experienced teachers are not surprised at all. They know this reality only too well. End-of-year survival concerns include a whole new set of issues: final grading, maintaining permanent records, recommendations for student placement in the next grade/subject, closing the school year, and whether the new teacher will be issued a contract for the following year. Helping new teachers anticipate that the spring is likely to bring a host of new questions about policies, practices, and procedures can be enormously reassuring to them and can prompt them to get necessary support during their weekly or biweekly mentor conversations. Knowing that they are not alone in their experience of the first year allows new teachers to devote more energy to teaching and less to being preoccupied with feelings of inadequacy, uncertainty, or isolation.

The complexities of teaching are immense, and it is a rare first-year teacher who doesn't experience some difficulty with the many challenges of meeting the needs of all students. Mentors who understand the typical phases new teachers move through and the types of concerns they will have can provide appropriately targeted, appropriately timed, effective support.

The Exploration of Excellent Teaching

Concerns about teachers who are not credentialed to teach the subjects they are teaching, coupled with low student achievement scores, have converged into one focal point: an urgent drive to improve teacher quality. Federal as well as many state-level policies and other initiatives emphasize the importance of enhancing teacher quality. However, teacher quality that is primarily defined by certification and licensure is an important but incomplete measure. Credentials do not make the teacher. What really matters is the quality of teaching that occurs daily within the classroom and throughout a teacher's career.

Much the same conclusion emerged from an extensive, international study that took place in conjunction with the Third International Mathematics and Science Study (TIMSS, now known as Trends in International Mathematics and Science Study). Through hundreds of classroom video samples, the study compared the teaching of eighth grade mathematics in Germany, Japan, and the United States (Stigler & Hiebert, 1999). The researchers found that U.S. mathematics lessons were overall more teacher-focused and less challenging for students as compared to lessons in the other countries. Based on their analysis of the international data, the researchers conclude, "Teaching, not teachers, is the critical factor.... Although variability in competence is certainly visible in the videos we collected, such differences are dwarfed by the differences in *teaching methods* that we see across cultures" (p. 10). One of their main recommendations for improving U.S. education is to "restructure schools as places where teachers can learn."

Mentoring can play a significant role in ensuring that schools are places where teachers as well as students can learn and where the newest teachers are inducted into a culture of continuous improvement focused on student learning.

What Excellent Teaching Looks Like

Promoting "high-quality teaching" requires first establishing a shared understanding of what is meant by the term. Several organizations and individuals have contributed in significant ways to developing the vocabulary that schools and teachers can use as a resource to build their understanding of high-quality teaching. The Interstate New Teachers Assessment and Support Consortium (INTASC) developed a set of standards to guide the certification and licensure of teachers. Similarly, the National Board of Professional Teaching Standards (NBPTS) developed teaching standards that define what it means and "looks like" to become a National Board Certified Teacher. Educational Testing Service (ETS) developed the Praxis III Teacher Assessment, which uses paper and pencil test items as well as practice-based assessments to measure teachers' content knowledge and pedagogical content knowledge.

In her book *Enhancing Professional Practice: A Framework for Teaching,* Charlotte Danielson integrated INTASC, NBPTS, and Praxis III standards in a framework for teaching that can serve as a touchstone for mentors, new teachers, administrators, and anyone interested in examining teaching and learning. This framework has been used across the country and abroad for several purposes, including reflection and self-assessment, mentoring and induction, peer coaching, and supervision and evaluation (Danielson, 1996, in press).

Danielson's framework for teaching outlines four primary domains of teaching and, within these domains, further describes 22 components (see figure 3.3).

This framework, informed by research, provides a useful perspective for conversations between mentors and new teachers about practice. In particular, the two most readily observable domains — Domain 2: The Classroom Environment and Domain 3: Instruction — can provide a focus for conversations, observations, and reflection on practice. Conversations between mentors and new teachers can focus on what each component of teaching practice would look like within a particular academic discipline. This framework for teaching is a powerful tool for keeping the focus of mentoring and induction on practice-based, content-specific reflection and self-assessment.

Across the research regarding effective teaching, there is general agreement on what high-quality, effective teaching looks like (Saphier & Gower, 1997; Danielson, 1996; Hunter, 1982) and the qualities that characterize excellent teachers. Excellent teachers do not view learning as a product that they alone can create but see themselves as facilitating and supporting their students' learning and helping them develop a sense of purpose and excitement. And excellent teachers never lose sight of student outcomes while they also maintain a student-centered classroom (WestEd, 2002; Bernhardt, 2000).

With a focus on what their students need, excellent teachers use data from formative and standardized assessments to differentiate instruction. They understand differences in student learning styles and backgrounds and, as much as possible, adapt instruction accordingly. They respect and value the cultural and ethnic distinctions that students bring to classroom life and seek to understand their students' perspectives, exhibiting genuine interest in students' cultures of origin and modeling an appreciation of diverse cultures. For all their students, excellent teachers recognize the importance of self-esteem and nurture it in ways that are authentic and promote growth.

With their deep content and content-related pedagogical knowledge, excellent teachers design and implement standards-based lessons. They are able to anticipate student misconceptions about particular content, plan ways to address them, and maintain high expectations for all their students. As communicators, they are clear and appropriate whether interacting with students, administrators, or parents.

As learners and models for their students, excellent teachers demonstrate a mind-set of continual curiosity — in both subject matter and pedagogy — throughout their work lives. They are thoughtful risk-takers and encourage students to be so as well. They are open to trying out new strategies and approaches to continually refine their practice.

Presumably, in the course of coming to a shared understanding about the elements of excellent teaching, a mentor and new teacher pair will recognize that they share consonant teaching philosophies even though they may differ on particular teaching approaches. This is an important baseline for any mentoring partnership.

How Mentors and New Teachers Explore Excellent Teaching

With a shared understanding of what excellent teaching looks like, the mentor and the new teacher will then want to incorporate reflective practice into their relationship. They must engage in conversations about teaching and do so often. Through such talk and reflection, the mentoring pair will be able to move from knowing about their practice to being more explicit and conscious about what they are doing, why, and how it relates to goals for student learning.

FIGURE 3.3: COMPONENTS OF PROFESSIONAL PRACTICE

Domain 1: Planning and Preparation

Component 1a: Demonstrating Knowledge of Content and Pedagogy

Knowledge of content and the structure of the discipline

Knowledge of prerequisite relationships

Knowledge of content-related pedagogy

Component 1b: Demonstrating Knowledge of Students

Knowledge of child and adolescent development

Knowledge of the learning process

Knowledge of students' skills, knowledge, and language proficiency

Knowledge of students' interests and cultural heritage

Knowledge of students' special needs

Component 1c: Selecting Instructional Goals

Value, sequence, and alignment

Clarity

Balance

Suitability for diverse learners

Component 1d: Demonstrating Knowledge of Resources

Resources for classroom use

Resources to extend content knowledge and pedagogy

Resources for students

Component 1e: Designing Coherent Instruction

Learning activities

Instructional materials and resources

Instructional groups

Lesson and unit structure

Component 1f: Assessing Student Learning

Congruence with instructional outcomes

Criteria and standards

Design of formative assessments

Domain 2: The Classroom Environment

Component 2a: Creating an Environment of Respect and Rapport

Teacher interaction with students

Student interactions with one another

Component 2b: Establishing a Culture of Learning

Importance of the content

Expectations for learning and achievement

Students' pride in work

Component 2c: Managing Classroom Procedures

Management of instructional groups

Management of transitions

Management of materials and supplies

Performance of non-instructional duties

Supervision of volunteers and paraprofessionals

Component 2d: Managing Student Behavior

Expectations

Monitoring of student behavior

Response to student misbehavior

Components 2e: Organizing Physical Space

Safety and accessibility

Arrangement of furniture and use of physical resources

48

Domain 3: Instruction

Component 3a: Communicating With Students

Expectations for learning

Directions and procedures

Explanations of content

Use of oral and written language

Component 3b: Using Questioning and Discussion Techniques

Quality of questions

Discussion techniques

Student participation

Component 3c: Engaging Students in Learning

Activities and assignments

Grouping of students

Instructional materials and resources

Structure and pacing

Component 3d: Using Assessment in Instruction

Assessment criteria

Monitoring of student learning

Feedback to students

Student self-assessment and monitoring of progress

Component 3e: Demonstrating Flexibility and Responsiveness

Lesson adjustment

Response to students

Persistence

Domain 4: Professional Responsibilities

Component 4a: Reflecting on Teaching

Accuracy

Use in future teaching

Component 4b: Maintaining Accurate Records

Student completion of assignments

Student progress in learning

Non-instructional records

Component 4c: Communicating with Families

Information about the instructional program

Information about individual students

Engagement of families in the instructional program

Component 4d: Participating in a Professional Community

Relationships with colleagues

Involvement in a culture of professional inquiry

Service to the school

Participation in school and district projects

Component 4e: Growing and Developing Professionally

Enhancement of content knowledge and pedagogical skill

Receptivity to feedback from colleagues

Service to the profession

Component 4f: Showing Professionalism

Integrity and ethical conduct

Service to students

Advocacy

Decision making

Note. From *Enhancing Professional Practice: A Framework for Teaching*, by C. Danielson, 1996, Alexandria, VA: Association for Supervision and Curriculum Development. Copyright 1996 by Association for Supervision and Curriculum Development. Reprinted with permission.

Mentors help new teachers ask themselves questions such as those in figure 3.4, and they also encourage an inquiry perspective by serving as role models. Effective mentors demonstrate ongoing intellectual exploration — for example, by reading educational research journals, attending professional conferences, directing new teachers to sources of information, and discussing research with new teachers and its implications for classroom life. Through their own continuing inquiry into research on excellent teaching, mentor teachers also become an invaluable resource for new teachers.

FIGURE 3.4: QUESTIONS FOR THE REFLECTIVE PRACTITIONER

Excellent teachers are committed to a self-determined fine-tuning of their craft. In a mentoring partnership, teachers might investigate questions such as the following:

- How much instructional time am I spending on the content area(s) that I am teaching?

- What effect is the time spent having on student learning and achievement? What is my evidence?

- How, if at all, do my personal preferences and/or comfort levels affect how much time I spend on certain concepts and/or content?

- What type of verbal interactions do I have with students? Are these interactions instructional, or are most of my communications with students focused on classroom procedures? How much do I probe for deeper understanding?

- How well is my philosophy of teaching aligned with my actions in my classroom?

Action research is another powerful way for mentors to model professional learning. Action research sets into motion a cycle of systematic inquiry in which teachers identify, study, and answer questions and, as a result, develop new questions to explore. Teachers who participate in action research projects become more flexible in their thinking, more receptive to new ideas, and more able to solve problems as they arise (Oja & Smulyan, 1989). New teachers are more apt to become involved in action research if they see it modeled by their mentors and if they have the opportunity to discuss it with their mentors.

CONSIDER THIS

Action research is a powerful professional development strategy to promote teacher reflection and changes in classroom practice. However, we suggest waiting until new teachers are in their second or third year of teaching before inviting them to become active participants in action research projects.

The process of becoming an excellent teacher is an ongoing journey. While teachers achieve many milestones along the way, there is no final destination. For new teachers, most of what they do, plan, and think about each day will be new. For mentors, working with new teachers actually adds new dimensions to their own practice as they consider what they do and better ways to increase student achievement.

A School Culture That Supports Excellent Teaching

If teachers are to achieve excellence, they must be able to go through experiences of trial and error — taking risks (within certain acceptable parameters) and reflecting on what worked, what didn't work, and why. Schools and districts can help in several ways to promote teachers' reflection on and improvement of their practice.

First, teachers must have time to talk about and reflect on their teaching. As adults, we do not learn from experience alone but through a combination of experience and reflection upon that experience (Dewey, 1933). Mentors and new teachers require many opportunities for focused, reflective conversations about teaching and learning (Schön, 1990). As teachers become more skilled at reflecting on their practice through personal reflection and conversations with colleagues, they also become better able to respond to "teachable moments," adjusting their teaching to best serve a particular need at the exact moment the need is being presented — for example, by altering a planned lesson to accommodate a compelling student observation or jumping ahead several lessons because a group of learners "got it" quicker than anticipated. This responsiveness is another form of "reflective practice," which schools can support by providing teachers with time for talking about teaching and learning.

Second, school cultures should value instructional risk-taking as a way to promote the development of excellent teaching. In concert with opportunities for taking risks, new teachers need opportunities for reflecting on and understanding why something did or did not work. The school and individual mentors must encourage the kind of creativity that risk-taking represents and then support it with sufficient time for new teachers to analyze why something they tried did or did not succeed. Administrators and school board members should express their support for instructional risk-taking explicitly and often. Mentors should continually promote risk-taking dispositions in their conversations with new teachers. Schools could demonstrate how they value risk-taking by altering the evaluation process during the time when a teacher is employing a particular innovation. We often stress that new teachers should teach directly from the curriculum materials initially, reflect on that experience, and then make evidence-based modifications. Typically, those

51

modifications will continue to evolve over a teacher's career as he or she encounters new students and new evidence and takes new risks.

Third, the notion of excellent teaching must be articulated in relationship to student learning outcomes. Excellent teachers make decisions about what they teach and how they teach based on what they want their students to know, do, and be like. Similarly, they model what they expect of their students. For example, a teacher who models high self-esteem can have a positive effect on the self-esteem of his or her students. There is a strong and positive connection between the development of adults and of children in schools (Levine, 1999), so when teachers acquire and employ the building blocks of excellent teaching, positive effects on student learning result.

Lastly, practitioners need to be encouraged to explore the research on excellent and effective teaching in their own classrooms. By actively testing the current knowledge base of excellent teaching, teachers formulate an individual philosophy regarding their craft and recognize the importance of carrying out their work in the context of an effective school. Teachers thrive in a school culture that recognizes, fosters, and encourages the continuum of teacher development, honors teachers in all stages of their professional growth, and provides time and organizational structures for collaborative efforts focused on individual development as well as development of the relevant supportive systems within a school or district (Feiman-Nemser, 2001).

chapter FOUR

Preparing Mentor Teachers as Collaborative Coaches

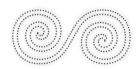

Dancers have mirrors. Where are our mirrors? The light in the eyes of the students is not enough.

– Pat Wolfe (in Hill and Hawk, 1999)

When teachers, like dancers, have the necessary mirrors, they are able to check actual performance against their intended plan and are able to better understand where and when to make adjustments. Mentors can provide "mirrors" for new teachers through collaborative coaching and other practices that support reflection. This chapter introduces the collaborative coaching cycle — the lesson planning conversation, coaching observation and gathering of data, and the reflecting conversation — that mentors use to provide new teachers with opportunities to become increasingly intentional about their instruction.

The Intentional Teacher

When mentors act as collaborative coaches, they support new teachers to become intentional in their practice, to develop and combine a deep understanding of instructional theory with skillful implementation. Figure 4.1 depicts what is involved in being intentional about instruction.

FIGURE 4.1: THE WINDOW INTO TEACHER THINKING

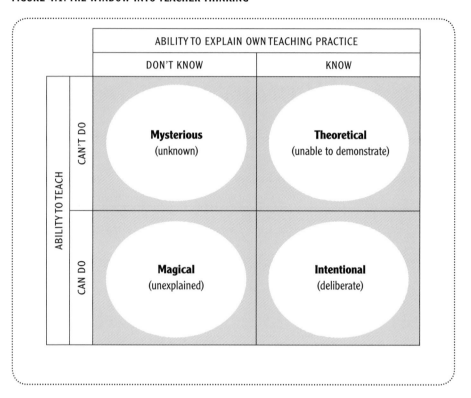

Note. From *Mentoring: A Resource and Training Guide for Educators,* by A. Newton et al., 1994, San Francisco: WestEd. Copyright 1994 by WestEd. Adapted with permission.

For teachers who do not understand or have the ability to perform a specific aspect of teaching, the teaching is *mysterious* (unknown).

When teachers can understand or explain a specific instructional strategy, but lack the ability to perform it, their understanding is *theoretical* (unable to demonstrate). For instance, teachers may be able to explain what an inquiry lesson should be like but cannot implement such a lesson.

Conversely, when teachers are able to teach in a particular way (even masterfully), but are unable to articulate their reasons for why they do so, we refer to this situation as *magical* (unexplained). Such teachers operate on intuition or may not remember what they figured out a long time ago. They may explain their practice in words such as, "I've been teaching for 25 years. I just teach."

When teachers know what they are teaching, why they are teaching it in particular ways for particular groups of students, what they would do differently (or keep) the next time and why, these teachers are *intentional* (deliberate) about their practice.

Effective mentors are deliberate in their use of various coaching approaches to enhance new teachers' intentionality and help them move toward becoming excellent teachers. Mentors consciously match their coaching approaches to the specific needs of new teachers for structure, direction, or guidance. They may employ a nondirective, a collaborative, or a direct informational approach when working with new teachers. The nondirective approach is most suited to helping new teachers "self-coach," but mentors must draw on all three approaches and choose the most appropriate for a given situation.

CONSIDER THIS:

As instructional leaders, mentors use focused reflection on lesson planning, implementation, and student assessment to coach new teachers in becoming more intentional about their practice. Teachers who are intentional about their practice know what they did, why they did it, what they would do differently (or keep) the next time, and why.

Norms of Collaboration: Essential Skills for Collaborative Dialogue

Whether engaging in conversations about new teachers' planning of a lesson, discussing the observation data in reflecting conversations, or interacting during more informal encounters, certain norms of collaboration (Garmston & Wellman, 2002) assure effective communication between mentors and new teachers. These norms, described in figure 4.2, are skills that most educators have and apply on a daily basis. To carry out effective dialogue, mentors and new teachers need to use these skills consistently and consciously, so that they become norms of behavior even when circumstances are less than ideal or when their "buttons are pushed."

FIGURE 4.2: THE SEVEN NORMS OF COLLABORATION

Pausing

Pausing before responding or asking a question allows time for thinking and enhances dialogue, discussion, and decision-making.

Paraphrasing

Using a paraphrase starter that is comfortable for you — "So…" or "As you are saying…" or "You are thinking…" — and following the starter with a paraphrase lets the new teacher know that you understand and/or are seeking to further understand what he or she is really saying.

Probing

Using gentle, open-ended probes or inquiries, such as "Please say more…" or "I'm curious about…" or "I'd like to hear more about that…" increases the clarity and precision of the new teacher's thinking.

Putting ideas on the table

Ideas are at the heart of meaningful dialogue. Label the intention of your comments. For example, you might say, "Here is one idea…" or "One thought I have is…" or "Here is a possible approach…." This norm also includes knowing when to take ideas off the table.

Paying attention to self and others

Meaningful dialogue between a mentor and a new teacher is facilitated when the speaker is aware not only of what she or he is saying but also of how it is said and how the listener is responding. This norm includes paying attention to learning style when planning for and engaging in conversations.

Presuming positive intentions

Assuming that the other partner's intentions are positive promotes trust and meaningful dialogue. Statements that might otherwise be perceived as put-downs are discounted and the focus remains on communication about ideas. Using positive intentions in one's speech is a manifestation of this norm.

Pursuing a balance between advocacy and inquiry

All of the other norms can to be used in service of this foundational norm. Pursuing and maintaining a balance between advocating for a position and inquiring into one's own and others' positions positively impacts the learning and collegiality of the mentoring partnership.

Note. From *The Adaptive School: Developing and Facilitating Collaborative Groups Syllabus*, by R. Garmston and B. Wellman, 2002, El Dorado Hills, CA: Center for Adaptive Schools. Copyright 2002 by Center for Adaptive Schools: http://www.adaptiveschools.com. Adapted with permission.

The seven norms of collaboration promote the skills of active listening. A teacher who is actively listening uses appropriate silence and wait time, demonstrates congruent body language, and acknowledges what the other person is saying by paraphrasing, summarizing, interpreting, or inferring.

An important aspect of active listening is to ask follow-up questions that probe for specificity. Probing for specificity can be especially valuable during a planning conversation. The mentor must not assume that a new teacher's initial responses will adequately answer the mentor's questions about the lesson. For example, when asked to identify the objective of the lesson, a new teacher might respond, "To teach multiplication." Other than knowing that the lesson will focus on mathematical multiplication, there is no clarity about the teacher's objective. Figure 4.3 demonstrates how a mentor might probe further. Through cycles of pausing, paraphrasing, and asking probing questions, the mentor can assist the new teacher in thinking through and identifying the specific objective of the lesson. The mentor's questions also prompt the new teacher to begin to talk and think about how the new teacher would know that the students "got it."

FIGURE 4.3: PROBING FOR SPECIFICITY: AN EXAMPLE

Mentor: What is the objective of this lesson you are planning?

New Teacher: To teach multiplication.

Mentor: What will you teach about multiplication?

New Teacher: Well, we've been working with multiplying two- and three-digit numbers. Some of the students are having difficulty in working the algorithm.

Mentor: How are you thinking of addressing that?

New Teacher: I thought I would provide some examples of area models using graph paper so that they could deconstruct and reconstruct the numbers they are multiplying. I think if they can see that 35 x 25 can also be described as (30 x 20) + (30 x 5) + (5 x 20) + (5 x 5), it might help them to better understand how to work the algorithm.

Mentor: So, you want to help students concretely visualize the operation of multiplication by separating place value?

New Teacher: Exactly.

Mentor: How will you know that they have increased their understanding?

New Teacher: Well, I will ask them to create several area models on graph paper as well as to work the examples using the standard algorithm, and then I will collect and review their work.

Active listening is a skill that many teachers do quite well. Yet even when people want to be fully present as listeners, they may experience a tendency toward "ego speak" — responding to an experience that someone else is recounting by recalling a similar personal experience. Ego speakers cannot wait until the other person is finished so that they can share: "Well, that's interesting, but wait until you hear what happened to me...." Of course, it can be appropriate at times for the mentor to tell stories that are informative to the new teacher, but the tendency toward ego speak becomes a problem whenever the story-telling shifts the focus too much onto the mentor and interferes with the new teacher's own reflective thought.

CONSIDER THIS

A good rule of thumb is to ask oneself, "Am I telling this story because it will it be helpful to the listener or because I have a need to tell it?"

60

Ego speak can be especially problematic when someone of greater experience is assisting someone of lesser experience. The temptation to succumb to ego speak is hard to fight when the more experienced person, out of deep caring and concern, wants to "fix the problem." However, jumping in rather than pausing is a lost opportunity for the mentor to allow the brilliance of the new teacher to shine through.

The Collaborative Coach

By employing skills of active listening and the norms of collaboration, mentors act as instructional leaders and hold up mirrors for new teachers through continuous cycles of collaborative coaching.

Promoting colleagues' reflection on their practice is the greatest gift mentors can give. In the words of one observer,

> [Reflection is] an active process of witnessing one's own experience in order to take a closer look at it, sometimes to direct attention to it briefly, but often to explore it in greater depth.... In the world of work, there are enormous opportunities to learn, yet relatively few structures that support learning from experience. (Amulya, 2003)

Mentoring programs for new teachers have the potential to provide such a structure by institutionalizing the practice of reflection. Reflection, as a process of inquiry, is how mentors facilitate thought and growth, both for the new teachers and for themselves. To promote productive reflection for new teachers, mentors must learn to be effective at collaborative coaching. Mentors are chosen because they are excellent teachers with the disposition to support the learning of others — peers as well as students. Being an excellent teacher is different from being a collaborative coach for new teachers.

To coach is to meet colleagues where they are and explicitly support them in achieving the goals they set for themselves. Effective coaching of new teachers depends on mentors having positive presuppositions about them. First of all, mentors must believe that new teachers want to do a good job. Mentors also must assume that new teachers have the capacity to identify their challenges and to grow. Finally, mentors must trust in new teachers' willingness to engage in supportive reflection about their practice.

As collaborative coaches, mentors promote reflection about specific aspects of lessons as well as about larger issues of pedagogy and curriculum. By gathering data that new teachers request, mentors help new teachers consider objective evidence about their effectiveness with students and enable them thereby to make more informed decisions about their practice.

61

As adult learners, new teachers require opportunities to make sense of new knowledge, skills, and experience through their own eyes and through their own reflection. Collaborative coaches guide rather than direct new teachers toward focused reflection on their teaching practice. Through this process of guided reflection on practice, new teachers deepen their ability to be intentional in their teaching. No amount of telling on the part of the coach can substitute for the value and essential nature of self-discovery by the new teacher.

The Collaborative Coaching Model

The collaborative view of coaching incorporates the thinking, research, and practice of several others over the years, especially with regard to promoting reflection and providing feedback to new teachers (Costa & Garmston, 2002; Glickman, 2002; Saphier & Gower, 1997; Acheson & Gall, 1987; Hunter, 1982; Goldhammer, Anderson, & Krajewski, 1980).

The collaborative coaching model presented here builds from the groundbreaking work of Art Costa and Robert Garmston and their development and subsequent enhancements of Cognitive Coaching.[SM] The Cognitive Coaching[SM] approach focuses on applying specific coaching strategies in order to mediate teacher thinking in ways that lead to explicit and overt changes in teaching practice that are known to create greater student learning and achievement. Shifts in teacher thinking and behavior are facilitated by repeated cycles of planning, coaching observation and data gathering, and reflecting (Costa & Garmston, 2002).

Additionally, the collaborative coaching model includes the dimensions of mutual reflection on teaching practice and an explicit emphasis on intentionality for new teachers and mentors alike. Through ongoing collaborative dialogue, mentor and new teacher pairs engage in meta-reflection and analysis of their practice. (See figure 4.4 for a graphic representation of the collaborative coaching model.)

FIGURE 4.4: A COLLABORATIVE COACHING MODEL

Student's
Growth, Learning, and Achievment

Consistent and Differentiated
instructional behaviors

Intentionality
in teaching, learning,
and assessing

COACH

NEW TEACHER

Coach's and New Teacher's
Reflective Questioning and
Data Gathering

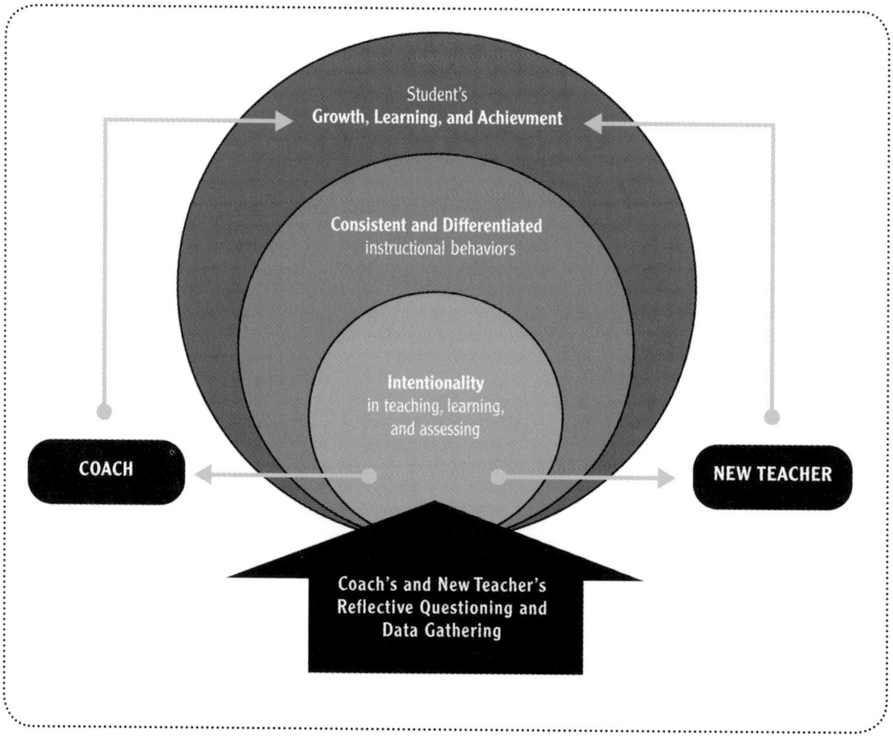

Even though mentors are primarily focused on supporting new teachers to become more intentional in their practice, by engaging in multiple cycles of planning and reflecting conversations about new teachers' practice mentors naturally reflect on their own practice as well. Often this opportunity to have conversations about new teachers' practice contributes to mentors' shift from *magical* (unexplained) teaching — being able to teach, even masterfully, without the ability to explain their teaching — to a place of intentionality, from which mentors can consistently and explicitly explain the reasoning for their teaching behaviors and decision-making. When mentors display masterful teaching without the ability to explain why they do what they do, new teachers can interpret the mentors' teaching ability as "magic" and may feel as though they could never reach the same level of mastery. On the other hand, when mentors are able to explain the reasons for their teaching decisions, new teachers are able to see clear connections between teaching behaviors and the impact of those behaviors on students. This, in turn, helps new teachers become more intentional in their teaching.

As mentor and new teacher pairs become comfortable in the collaborative coaching cycle, it may be possible to make videotaped recordings of planning conversations, classroom lessons, and reflective conversations for focused use in a study group with other mentors. The opportunity to reflect on coaching allows mentors to "think about their thinking" as coaches, just as the coaching process affords them with an opportunity to "think about their thinking" as teachers. When mentors have the opportunity to reflect on their coaching in these ways, they are able to increase their intentional use of coaching approaches and behaviors.

CONSIDER THIS

When videotaping classroom lessons, it is essential to secure signed permission from parents or guardians of the children who are in the classroom being videotaped. Most schools secure such permission as standard procedure and have forms to use for this purpose. In any case, prior to videotaping any classroom make sure that signed permissions have been obtained for each child.

The Collaborative Coaching Cycle

The three phases in the coaching cycle — the planning conversation, coaching observation and data gathering, and the reflecting conversation — all have the ultimate goal of enhancing intentional instruction. Figure 4.5 illustrates these relationships.

The collaborative coaching process is intended to be iterative, occurring again and again during the mentor-new teacher relationship. It would be optimal to have a coaching cycle every month. If this is not possible, we recommend that each mentoring partnership undertake at least four coaching cycles per year.

FIGURE 4.5: THE COACHING CYCLE

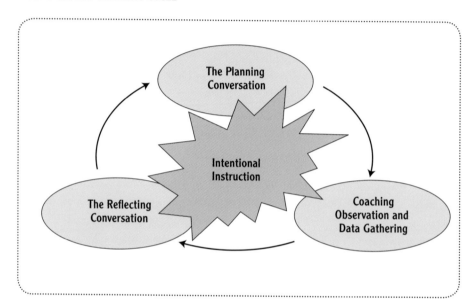

The Planning Conversation

All phases of the coaching cycle are important, but an effective planning conversation is essential for maximizing the help coaches can provide. In a planning conversation, the mentor asks the new teacher to go through a trial run of exactly what will be taught to the students and what the teacher expects students will learn. By asking effective questions, the mentor facilitates a process through which the new teacher will have already taught the lesson, in a sense, before ever entering the classroom. Even if the mentor never observes the lesson, the new teacher may have thought through potential obstacles and made adjustments ahead of time because of a planning conversation that was done well.

In a planning conversation, the main challenge for mentors is to assist new teachers to make explicit their intentions for the lesson. New teachers must be able to articulate how they will know that each student "gets it." Additionally, they need to verbalize the relationship between teaching behavior, expected student behavior, lesson objectives, and desired outcomes.

Mentors can meet this challenge by including particular components in each planning conversation. Specifically, effective planning conversations provide opportunities for new teachers to refine and rehearse a lesson, including to accomplish the following:

- clarify goals and objectives;
- identify what they will teach and how they will teach it;
- determine routines, procedures, and materials management;
- determine what evidence will let them know that students understand and are learning;
- decide what types of data will be useful to have for reflecting upon the lesson afterward; and
- run through the lesson once before actually teaching it to their students.

Mentors can use specific questions to probe any of these areas. The list in figure 4.6 provides a number of examples.

FIGURE 4.6: POSSIBLE QUESTIONS FOR THE PLANNING CONVERSATION

Questions to clarify goals

- What are you planning to teach?

- What do you want students to know and be able to do as a result of this lesson?

- Which curriculum standard(s) does this lesson address?

- How does this fit with what you have been doing recently with your students?

Questions to identify what will be taught and how it will be taught

- What specifically will you be introducing/reviewing with the students? How will you do that?

- Do any of your students have special needs? If so, how will you accommodate them?

- What, if any, modifications do you need to make for your students? How will you provide for those accommodations?

- What will I see when I observe the beginning of the lesson? The middle? The end?

- What will you be doing?

- What will the students be doing?

- What is the most crucial ingredient for this lesson to be successful?

- What, if any, concerns do you have? How will you address them?

Questions on routines, procedures, and materials management

- How many students do you have?

- How will the students be organized — for example, individually? In groups?

- What are the benefits of organizing the students in this way?

- How long is the lesson?

- What, if any, materials will the students be using? How will you distribute them?

Questions on evidence of student understanding and learning

- How will you know if students have learned what you want them to know and be able to do?

- What specific evidence are you looking for?

- How will you be assessing this lesson?

- In the future, how will you assess learning in this lesson — for example, as it relates to other lessons in the unit?

Questions regarding what data will be most useful to reflect upon

- What would you like me to pay attention to?

- What kind of information would be most useful for you to reflect upon after the lesson?

- What way of recording that information would be most useful to you?

Reminder for the new teacher

- Remember that if you need to change anything for the benefit of the students, feel free to do so. That is a natural part of teaching.

Mentors often share questions such as those in figure 4.6 with new teachers prior to the planning conversation so that they may be prepared to answer them. Providing sample questions ahead of time helps new teachers think about lesson planning and implementation even before the planning conversation. As a result, they are better prepared and may begin to integrate these questions in their planning of other lessons.

When arranging a time and place for the planning conversation, it is important to think about issues of privacy, potential interruptions, and other distractions. The following guidelines apply:

- Plan enough time for the conversation (30–45 minutes at first; eventually 15–20 minutes is usually adequate).

- Choose a place where there will be no interruptions or other distractions.

- In case distractions do occur, except for issues of safety or other emergencies, make it clear that the planning conversation is a priority and do not allow the interruption to take precedence.

While the classroom is often the most convenient place to conduct a planning conversation, it may be that students typically come into the classroom for extra help during the time scheduled for the planning conversation. Such interruptions will be distracting to the new teacher and create a difficult situation for candid dialogue and reflection. Likewise, conducting a planning (or reflecting) conversation in the faculty lounge, when other colleagues may be coming in or out, is also inappropriate. In addition to the distraction of such interruptions, discussions that indicate uncertainty about a plan or concern about

67

something that may not have succeeded are in many school contexts viewed not as inquiry but as evidence of poor teaching. To avoid putting a new teacher in an uncomfortable position in front of colleagues, which could also compromise the mentor and new teacher relationship, it is essential that planning and reflecting conversations be held in a private location that assures confidentiality.

As a backdrop to the planning conversation, the mentor must understand a variety of teaching strategies and when and why they are useful. During the planning conversation, the mentor and new teacher prepare for the mentor to observe the new teacher's classroom. Together they need to agree upon the focus of the mentor's observation, what type of data will be gathered, and what method the mentor will use to gather the requested data. It is very likely that new teachers will not know what data are important to collect for a particular focus. The mentor may need to probe with follow-up questions to get at this information. Often, because new teachers lack experience with data gathering techniques and uses, the mentor may need to suggest which data will give the new teacher feedback about her or his area of interest or concern.

Following the planning conversation, the mentor should have a clear picture of what and how the new teacher intends to teach, any particular focus the new teacher may have (for example, what she or he wants the mentor to look for during the observation), and what method of data gathering to use during the observation.

CONSIDER THIS

When gathering observation data, it is very important that the mentor literally record whatever data are agreed upon in the planning conversation. Sticking to the plan of gathering data only and exactly as agreed upon validates the importance and relevance of the planning conversation and builds trust and rapport between the mentor and new teacher.

Coaching Observation and Data Gathering

Having prepared ahead of time with the new teacher, the mentor observes in the new teacher's classroom and gathers data that will be used as a basis for promoting the new teacher's reflection on his or her teaching practices. When mentors share data in an objective fashion, new teachers are able to look into a "mirror" that reflects certain aspects of what really transpired during their lessons. With data as the starting point for a conversation, no judgment is implied and no excuses need to be offered. The data are there for consideration.

Being able to share data objectively is an acquired skill. Mentors need to be aware of potential pitfalls. For example, they may convey opinions about the new teacher's classroom in more ways than through spoken language. Nonverbal communication can speak volumes. Body language, tone of voice, or facial expression can instantly unveil subjective judgments (see figure 4.7).

FIGURE 4.7: HOW SPEAKERS CONVEY THEIR MESSAGES

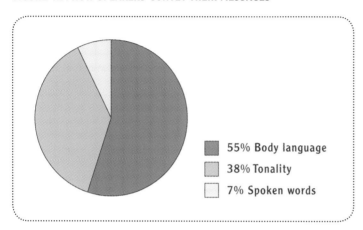

55% Body language
38% Tonality
7% Spoken words

Note. Data are from *Silent Messages: Implicit Communication of Emotions and Attitudes,* by A. Mehabrian (1980).

A mentor's observations in the new teacher's classroom may vary in length. However, a 10- to 15-minute observation is probably too short for the purpose of gathering useful data for the new teacher. When deciding how long a coaching observation should be, the mentor must always consider the verbal contract that was created during the planning conversation. Once the new teacher describes the lesson, outcomes, and objectives, the mentor has essentially "contracted" to observe the entire lesson. Mentors who leave the coaching observation prematurely can send a message of disapproval, indicating that the mentor saw something wrong or that the lesson was not really important. On the other hand, if the lesson is expected to be particularly long and the mentor knows that it will not be possible to stay the entire time, the mentor and new teacher need to agree during the planning conversation on when the mentor will leave.

Throughout the year, the mentor and new teacher will observe each other several times. How many coaching observations are enough will vary depending upon the specific needs of a new teacher. As noted, four formal coaching cycles are a minimum to support a new teacher's growth and reflection, but if a new teacher is struggling, additional coaching cycles may be necessary. And mentors and their partners may be in and out of each other's classrooms many times during the year for much shorter, less formal visits.

There are numerous methods of data gathering. Five of the most common and useful options include verbal flow, class traffic, selective verbatim, scripting, and audio or video recording.

Verbal Flow. In this technique, the observer records on a seating plan the number of teacher responses and questions to the whole class and to particular students, the number of responses per student, which students are being responded to by the teacher, and which students are talking to which other students.

This technique can provide useful data when new teachers want to know which students are involved in the lesson: which students they respond to and how often, whether they are responding to girls and boys equally or excluding any other group, or when they are concerned about any particular students.

Class Traffic. In this method, the observer uses a sketch of the classroom, including a labeled seating arrangement, to record where the teacher and students move during a lesson. With practice and experience, the class traffic technique can be used in conjunction with the Verbal Flow method described above.

The class traffic method is useful when the teacher is interested in data about his or her interactions with individual students or groups or to provide data that can help answer concerns about whether the teaching is directed more to one side of the room than the other, for example, or whether the teacher is connecting with all of the students during a lesson.

Selective Verbatim. In this technique, the observer records verbatim anything said by the teacher and students within a particular category. The category of verbal responses to be recorded is predetermined by the mentor and new teacher. For example, the new teacher may be interested in what type of questions she or he asks. The mentor would then record verbatim all of the questions that the new teacher asks. In another instance, the new teacher may be interested in knowing whether she or he favors one group over another with higher-level questions. In this case, the teacher could review the verbatim record of all questions to determine the distribution by group of higher-level questions. The teacher may want to know whether she or he is clear when giving directions; a transcript could reveal much about the new teacher's direction-giving exchanges with students.

This technique provides useful data if new teachers are interested in thinking about their questioning or direction-giving techniques, levels of student thinking, or amount of teacher talk.

Scripting. Scripting is a verbatim record of what was said by whom during a lesson. While data gathered by this method are extremely useful in providing an exact and objective account of what happened during a lesson, observers generally need several practice sessions before they are comfortable using this technique. The scripting method requires a very focused observer. However, its benefits are as great as the intensity of effort required to gather data in this way.

This technique can be used for whatever a teacher may want to know about what happened during the lesson, with the exception of class traffic patterns. After using the scripting technique to gather data, the mentor can ask the new teacher what he or she recalls thinking about when asking a certain question or when a particular student gave a specific response.

CONSIDER THIS

The task of recording data while observing a new teacher's classroom is demanding and requires an intense level of focus. Mentors often find that using a laptop computer to record agreed-upon data increases accuracy and speed.

71

Audio or Video Recording. Recordings can be used to gather data in response to anything the new teacher may be concerned about or interested in knowing — to record, for example, a particular part or aspect of a lesson, what is happening in the entire classroom during a lesson, or interactions between the teacher and a particular student or group of students. Recordings can also capture the behavior of students not involved with the teacher during a certain part of the lesson.

It is very important for mentors to consider the potentially intimidating nature of audio or video recording. Many new teachers may not be comfortable having someone record their lessons, particularly at the beginning of the school year or when they have not had previous experience with these data gathering methods. Often the mentor can help ease concerns by making it clear that the recording immediately becomes the property of the new teacher and will be shared with the mentor or other colleagues only if the recorded teacher so decides.

Alternatively, the mentor may suggest that the new teacher record his or her own lessons solely for personal viewing or listening, thereby allowing the new teacher to keep the data private. The mentor can give the new teacher a data gathering sheet with an explanation of how to use it and then let the new teacher practice. If new teachers are nervous about being observed or having their lesson recorded, this approach can often help curb that anxiety. Ultimately, it is the choice of the new teacher whether or not to be videotaped or audiotaped by the mentor teacher.

Figure 4.8 provides an overview of these strategies and when to use them.

FIGURE 4.8: CLASSROOM DATA GATHERING STRATEGIES

When looking for...	Use the following strategy
• Involvement of students in the lesson • What is happening with a certain group of students • Gender or other bias (which students are called on, how often, in what order)	**Verbal Flow** The observer records who talks to whom (e.g., which students the teacher calls on and how often, which students talk to which other students).
• Individualized instruction • Teacher connection to students throughout a lesson • Teacher proximity to students • Student behavior	**Class Traffic** The observer tracks the movement of the teacher around the classroom and identifies (by numbering the interactions) which students or groups the teacher interacts with.
• Students' level of thinking • Amount of teacher talk • What is happening with a certain group of students • Types of questions the teacher asks	**Selective Verbatim** The observer makes a written record of exactly what is said within a predetermined category in the classroom (e.g., teacher questions, student questions, student responses, teacher responses).
• Complete transcript of what occurred during a lesson or part of a lesson	**Scripting** The observer makes a written record of everything that is said by the teacher and by students during a lesson or part of a lesson.
• Complete record of what occurred during a lesson that can be replayed or reviewed by the teacher	**Audio or Video Recording** The observer or teacher records (audio or video) the lesson, focusing on the aspect of the class in which the teacher is most interested.

Note. From *Another Set of Eyes: Techniques for Classroom Observation, Trainers Manual,* by K. Acheson, 1987, Alexandria, VA: Association for Supervision and Curriculum Development. Copyright 1987 by Keith A. Acheson. Adapted with permission.

When selecting a specific method for gathering data, the mentor must consider the new teacher's own development in addition to the new teacher's request for data about a certain aspect of a lesson. For example, if a new teacher wants to know which students she or he responds to and how often, the mentor could use a verbal flow technique. Four months later, this same teacher, now further along in her or his development, may still be curious about his or her responses to students. However, at this point it may be more useful to find out how she or he responds to students in terms of choice of language or level of questions asked. For this purpose, the mentor may use the selective verbatim or scripting technique to allow for a deeper analysis of how the teacher responds to students.

The Reflecting Conversation

A successful reflecting conversation provides objective data to new teachers, affording them a low-threat opportunity to analyze their performance and learn from it. As Taggart and Wilson (1998) point out, "Learning is not only dependent on what we see but how those observations are processed" (p. 60). The information collected through observing new teachers becomes a tool that mentors and new teachers use in the reflective process. The ensuing dialogue often becomes the beginning of the next planning conversation, as new teachers consider what to focus on given what they are learning about their teaching.

73

CONSIDER THIS

Maintaining an objective, nonjudgmental stance during the reflecting conversation is often more challenging than during the planning conversation. Effective coaches invite new teachers to read through the data gathered and to reflect upon what they noticed about their teaching; these coaches do not interpret the data for the new teachers. This challenge can become heightened when the coach has a different philosophy about the way a lesson could be taught. It is important to focus on the relationship between what the new teacher intended for the students to learn and what the students actually learned.

The mentor's primary concern in a reflecting conversation is to ask questions that promote the new teacher's reflections on practice. While these questions are sometimes coupled with sharing observation data, the mentor's questions in a reflecting conversation are often much broader, evolving also from what a new teacher has thought about and shared with the mentor. Figure 4.9 identifies the many ways that reflecting conversations serve new teachers — from helping them recall and understand what happened, to helping them analyze why something happened and how to use that information.

FIGURE 4.9: NEW TEACHER OPPORTUNITIES IN REFLECTING CONVERSATIONS

Reflecting conversations offer a range of ways that new teachers can benefit from the interaction. Mentors might encourage them to undertake any of the following:

- Summarize and reflect on what occurred during their lesson.
- Identify impressions and assessments of how the lesson went.
- Recall data supporting impressions or assessments.
- Compare what was planned with what actually occurred (teaching decisions and student learning).
- Infer how teaching decisions/behaviors impacted student learning.
- Reflect on new learning and insights and how they will inform future teaching.
- Identify what was useful with regard to the planning and reflective conversations and what, if anything, to do differently next time.

During reflecting conversations, mentors need to help new teachers engage in basic reflection as well as more complex reflection. Basic reflection refers to thinking about the "technical correctness" of a teacher's decisions and usually involves taking into account just one or two aspects of what happens in the classroom. More complex reflection involves considering more and subtler implications of a classroom situation, including moral and ethical dimensions, and not only whether a particular teaching decision was "correct" or not. While some teachers may think about the basic aspects of their response before they can think about the more complex implications of their response, both of these forms of reflection are important. In fact, there are times when the technical correctness of a basic response supersedes any other considerations. The scenarios in figure 4.10 demonstrate the usefulness of each response form and how they differ.

Verbal flow and class traffic are the data gathering methods most helpful in promoting basic, or technical, reflection. Techniques of selective verbatim, scripting, and audio or video recordings are useful for setting up complex reflection.

FIGURE 4.10: BASIC AND COMPLEX FORMS OF REFLECTION

Juanita: Basic Reflection Then Complex Reflection

Juanita has trouble paying attention. Today she has been chatting during an entire lesson. Her teacher, Mr. Grove, reflects on what he can do. First he thinks of a basic response to the problem. Recognizing that Juanita pays more attention when he is closer to where she is sitting, he considers moving her seat near to his work space. Then he thinks of a complex response incorporating the fact that Juanita is new in the school and has few friends. He realizes that moving her seat will also remove her from the few friends she has made. So, rather than move her seat and take her away from a comfortable peer situation, he decides to make sure to move around the classroom more during his lessons and to spend more time closer to Juanita.

Jamie: Complex Reflection Then Basic Reflection

Ms. Rasthan has known that the practice fire drill would occur at 11:15 today. Her principal announced the fire drill at a faculty meeting three weeks earlier. It is almost 11:15 and she is finishing up a social studies lesson. She asks one last question. Jamie, who is very shy and unsure of herself, raises her hand to answer the question. Ms. Rasthan is thrilled at Jamie's willingness to share her opinion. Jamie begins to respond and is not finished when the fire drill sounds. Ms. Rasthan hesitates. Her complex response is to want to allow Jamie to continue — of all times to have to interrupt a student, and especially Jamie. However, a basic response is the appropriate one in this instance. Although this is a planned fire drill, there is always the possibility that it is the real thing. Ms. Rasthan knows that it is important that the students learn to respond immediately to the potential danger signaled by the alarm. She stops Jamie and asks the children to file out quietly.

Danny: Basic Reflection Then Complex Reflection

Ms. Dell had already spoken to Danny three times during the last 30 minutes of what she thought was a well-planned lesson. Once more his preoccupation with a particular math problem demanded her attention. Slightly flushed, she turned from the other students and fumed, "Danny, do you have anything to add?" Even though her pique was evident, happily Ms. Dell was saved from her basic response, one that would have reprimanded Danny for yet another interruption. Instead, almost before her question was complete, Danny blurted out, "Yes, I just figured out another way to do that one!" Minutes after the children had left for the day, Ms. Dell was at the children's conference table wondering why she knew that imposing a disciplinary measure was not the right response to Danny. Her reflection led her to the complex understanding that not only was Danny's learning process very discovery-oriented, but he also required opportunities to share his discoveries. Her challenge was to plan a way to meet Danny's needs that did not disadvantage the other students.

During the reflecting conversation, the mentor needs to refrain from an enthusiastic account of what she or he thought about the lesson. Praise is an ego booster, yet it does not always inform teaching practice. New teachers need to have opportunities to consider the data in such a way that they are able to reflect on their own lessons. Praise by the mentor can shut down the thinking of the new teacher, especially when the new teacher might have different feelings about the lesson. Similarly, if praise is given on one occasion and not on another, a new teacher may interpret the absence of praise as a negative value judgment. Praise is a form of judgment, and once a mentor begins judging the new teacher, the mentor will be expected to do so again.

Mentors can guide new teachers in addressing a range of topics when facilitating a reflecting conversation:

- impressions of the lesson based on recall;
- comparison of the lesson intent with what happened;
- inferences about the effect of teaching behaviors and/or decisions;
- how future teaching might be different; and
- how future coaching might be different.

Examples of specific questions to probe these topics are listed in figure 4.11.

CONSIDER THIS

While we have provided a fairly long list of questions as examples to use during the reflecting conversation, we encourage coaches to narrow the focus and limit the number of questions they ask. When asked too many questions, new teachers can feel overwhelmed or as though they are being "grilled." Quite often, a few well-framed questions serve as a welcomed invitation for new teachers to reflect aloud about how they thought their class went, what they liked, and what they might do differently next time.

FIGURE 4.11: POSSIBLE QUESTIONS FOR REFLECTING CONVERSATIONS

Questions to support summary of and reflection on the lesson, identification of impressions/assessments, and recall of data

- As you think back over the lesson, how would you describe what occurred?
- How do you think the lesson went? What causes you to say that?
- What did you notice about the students during the lesson?
- What evidence did you see that students were learning and understanding what you wanted them to?

Questions to support comparing the intent of the lesson with what occurred

- How did what occurred compare to what you had intended?
- Were there any surprises related to your teaching decisions? Related to student responses?

Questions to support inferences about how teaching behaviors and/or decisions impacted student learning

- What did you notice about your own thinking and decision-making during the lesson?
- How did your thinking and decision-making affect students?
- *(If applicable)* What was the effect of the shift you made from what you had intended?

Questions to support reflection on how new learning and insights will inform future practice

- What were the "keepers" during this lesson? What causes you to say that?
- What, if anything, would you change? What causes you to say that?
- What will you do as a follow-up to this lesson?
- As you reflect on this lesson, what other implications, if any, are there for what you will do in the future?

Questions about what was valuable and what could be improved about the coaching cycle

- What was most valuable and/or helpful to you?
- How could this process be improved to better serve your needs?

We are often asked about what a mentor should do if he or she notices during a coaching observation something of concern that was not part of the agreed-upon focus. Is it appropriate to mention this observation to the new teacher? Raising additional information during the reflecting conversation that had not been agreed upon during the planning conversation may well appear judgmental to the new teacher. In matters of safety or ethics, the mentor has a responsibility to raise the concern with the new teacher and an administrator, if necessary, just as the mentor would address safety or ethical concerns with any colleague. Otherwise, however, the mentor needs to limit the reflecting conversation to a consideration of the new teacher's requested data. If the mentor adds new topics to the reflecting conversation based on things the mentor became concerned about during the observation, the new teacher will lose faith in the coaching cycle as a safe and truly collaborative process.

An appropriate time to introduce other concerns that may have come up during the coaching observation is during the mentor-new teacher's weekly meeting. By introducing the topic as one of many issues discussed during these regular sessions, the mentor may promote the new teacher's reflection on the issue without conveying an evaluative judgment of a particular performance.

 As with the planning conversation, where and when the reflecting conversation is held can have a significant impact on its success. A reflecting conversation may be held any time from several hours to a few days following the actual coaching observation. Generally, however, the reflecting conversation should occur as soon after the observation as possible — but not immediately after. At the end of the observation, many mentors leave the observation data with new teachers. This way the new teacher is the keeper of the data and also has an opportunity to review and reflect on the data alone, prior to the reflecting conversation with the mentor. Mentors, too, need time for individual reflection in advance of the reflecting conversation. When both partners have such an opportunity before meeting, the reflecting conversation can be much more successful.

A mentor's primary role is to serve as a coach to support new teachers in becoming more intentional about their teaching. The wise mentor has deep knowledge and expertise but also knows when to keep that expertise in the background. Through deliberate application of coaching and communication skills, mentors develop trust and rapport with new teachers and provide them with a safe haven for taking risks, broadening their perspectives, and enhancing their teaching to support the learning and achievement of all students.

Conclusion

We have focused on the induction phase of teachers' careers, with an emphasis on ensuring that well-prepared mentors provide focused, content-specific support to new teachers. While we believe that mentoring and coaching are essential to teacher induction programs, we challenge the view that mentoring and coaching are important only during induction. If we are to create systems of support for teachers throughout their careers, mentoring and coaching need to begin during teacher preparation, extend through induction, and continue as an ongoing form of professional collaboration and learning. The preparation, induction, and career-long support of teachers deserves and requires a consolidated effort on the part of administrators, teacher leaders, teacher associations, higher education faculty, state education agency staff, and the range of professional development providers that serve our schools and districts.

We envision reflective teaching practice that is promoted through collaborative coaching as a central feature in all phases of teacher development. When teacher candidates, new teachers, mentors, lead mentors, administrators, and faculty from colleges and universities all reflect upon their teaching in ways that challenge the status quo, the goals of providing high-quality teachers in all classrooms and ensuring high-quality teaching for every child can be achieved. The learning strategies embodied in mentoring and collaborative coaching are at the heart of sustaining professional learning communities that share these goals.

Reference List

Acheson, K. A. (1987). *Another set of eyes: Techniques for classroom observation, Trainers manual.* Alexandria, VA: Association for Supervision and Curriculum Development.

Acheson, K., & Gall, M. (1987). *Techniques in the clinical supervision of teachers.* New York: Longman.

Amulya, J. (2003). *What is reflective practice?* Cambridge, MA: Center for Reflective Community Practice, Massachusetts Institute of Technology.

Bernhardt, V. (2000). New routes open when one type of data crosses another. *Journal of Staff Development, 21*(1), 33–37.

Bolich, A. M. (2001). *Reduce your losses: Help new teachers become veteran teachers.* Atlanta: Southern Regional Education Board (SREB).

Brackett, A. (2004). *Collaborative evaluation led by local educators: A practical, print-and web-based guide.* San Francisco: WestEd. Retrieved August 25, 2006, from http://www.neirtec.org/evaluation.

Cavell, L., Blank, R. K., Toye, C., & Williams, A. (2005). *Key state education policies on PK–12 education: 2004.* Washington, DC: Council of Chief State School Officers.

Costa, A. L., & Garmston, R. J. (2002). *Cognitive coaching: A foundation for Renaissance Schools* (2nd edition). Norwood, MA: Christopher-Gordon Publishers.

Danielson, C. (1996). *Enhancing professional practice: A framework for teaching.* Alexandria, VA: Association for Supervision and Curriculum Development.

Danielson, C. (in press). *Enhancing professional practice: A framework for teaching* (2nd edition). Alexandria, VA: Association for Supervision and Curriculum Development.

Darling-Hammond, L. (2000). *Solving the dilemmas of teacher supply, quality, and demand.* New York: National Commission on Teaching and America's Future.

Dewey, J. (1933). *How we think: A restatement of the relation of reflective thinking to the educative process* (2nd edition). New York: D.C. Heath

Feiman-Nemser, S. (2001). From preparation to practice: Designing a continuum to strengthen and sustain teaching. *Teachers College Record, 103*(6), 1013–1055.

Fideler, E. F., & Haselkorn, D. (1999). *Learning the ropes.* Belmont, MA; Recruiting New Teachers.

Garmston, R. J., & Wellman, B. M. (2002). *The adaptive school: Developing and facilitating collaborative groups syllabus.* El Dorado Hills, CA: Center for Adaptive Schools.

Glickman, C. (2002). *Leadership for learning: How to help teachers succeed.* Alexandria, VA: Association for Supervision and Curriculum Development.

Goldhammer, R., Anderson, R. H., & Krajewski, R. J. (1980). *Clinical supervision: Special methods for the supervision of teachers* (2nd edition). NewYork: Holt, Rinehart, and Winston.

Gordon, S. P., & Maxey, S. (2000). *How to help beginning teachers succeed.* Alexandria, VA: Association for Supervision and Curriculum Development.

Hill, J., & Hawk, K. (1999, August). *The powerful potential of research as a tool in change management.* Paper presented at the Innovation for Effective Schooling Conference, Auckland, Australia.

Hughes, G., Cowley, K. S., Copley, L. D., Finch, N. L., Meehan, M. L., Burns, R. C., Kusimo, P. S., Keyes, M. C., Orletsky, S. R., & Holdzkom, D. (2004). *Effects of a culturally responsive teaching project on teachers and students selected in Kanawha County, WV, Schools.* Charleston, WV: Edvantia.

Hunter, M. (1982). *Mastery Teaching.* El Segundo, CA: TIP Publications.

Ingersoll, R. M. (2001, January). A different approach to solving the teacher shortage problem. *Teaching Quality Policy Brief 3.* Center for the Study of Teaching and Policy.

Joyce, B., & Showers, B. (2002). *Student achievement through staff development* (3rd edition). Alexandria, VA: Association for Supervision and Curriculum Development.

Levine, S. L. (1999). *Promoting adult growth in schools: The promise of professional development.* Thousand Oaks, CA: Corwin Press.

Lindsey, R. B., Robins, K. N., & Terrell, R. D. (2003). *Cultural proficiency: A manual for school leaders.* Thousand Oaks, CA: Corwin Press.

Lipton, L., & Wellman, B. (2001). *Mentoring matters: A practical guide to learning-focused relationships.* Sherman, CT: Mira Via, LLC.

Mehrabian, A. (1980). *Silent messages: Implicit communication of emotions and attitudes.* Belmont, CA: Wadsworth Publishing Company.

Miller, P. A. (in press). *Mentoring in the learning community: Problematic practices and outcomes of initial implementation of formal mentoring programs in two New Hampshire school districts.* Doctoral dissertation, University of New Hampshire, Durham.

Moir, E. (1999). The stages of a teacher's first year. In M. Scherer (Ed.), *A better beginning: Supporting new teachers.* Alexandria, VA: Association for Supervision and Curriculum Development.

Moore-Johnson, S., & The Project on the Next Generation of Teachers. (2004). *Finders and keepers: Helping new teachers survive and thrive in our schools.* San Francisco: Jossey-Bass.

National Center for Education Statistics. (2001). *Attrition of new teachers among recent college graduates: Comparing occupational stability among 1992-93 college graduates who taught and those who worked in other occupations.* Washington, DC: U. S. Department of Education.

National Commission on Mathematics and Science Teaching for the 21st Century. (1999). *Before it's too late.* Washington, DC: Author.

Nave, B. (2004). Northern New England CoMentoring Network (NNECN) year three findings. *NNECN Annual Report to the National Science Foundation.* Augusta, ME: Maine Mathematics and Science Alliance.

Nave, B. (2006). *Northern New England CoMentoring Network (NNECN) final evaluation report.* Cambridge, MA: TERC.

Neufeld, B., & Roper, D. (2004). *Coaching: A strategy for developing instructional capacity.* Washington, DC: The Aspen Institute Program on Education; and Providence, RI: The Annenberg Institute for School Reform.

Newton, A., Bergstrom, K., Brennan, N., Dunne, K., Gilbert, C., Ibarguen, N., Perez-Selles, M., & Thomas, E. (1994). *Mentoring: A resource and training guide for educators.* San Francisco: WestEd.

Noddings, N. (1984). *Caring: A feminine approach to morals and ethics in education.* Berkeley: University of California Press.

Norton, M. S. (1999). Teacher retention: Reducing costly teacher turnover. *Contemporary Education, 70*(3), 52–55.

Odell, S. J., & Huling, L. (2000). *Quality mentoring for novice teachers.* Indianapolis, IN: Kappa Delta Pi.

Oja, S. N., & Smulyan, L. (1989). *Collaborative action research: A developmental approach.* Philadelphia: Falmer Press.

Peske, H. G., & Haycock, K. (2006, June). *Teaching inequality: How poor and minority students are shortchanged on teacher quality.* Washington, DC: The Education Trust. Retrieved August 25, 2006, from http://www2.edtrust.org/EdTrust/Press+Room/teacherquality2006.htm.

Public Agenda. (2000). *A sense of calling: Who teaches and why.* New York: Author.

Reiman, A. J., & Thies-Sprinthall, L. (1998). *Mentoring and supervision for teacher development.* Upper Saddle River, NJ: Addison Wesley Longman.

Saphier, J., & Gower, R. (1997). *The skillful teacher.* Carlisle, MA: Research for Better Teaching.

Schön, D. (1990). *Educating the reflective practitioner.* San Francisco: Jossey-Bass.

Shea, G. F. (1992). *Mentoring: A practical guide.* Menlo Park, CA: Crisp Publications.

Smith, T. M., & Ingersoll, R. M. (2004). What are the effects of induction and mentoring on beginning teacher turnover? *American Educational Research Journal, 41*(3), 681–714.

Stigler, J. W., & Hiebert, J. (1999). *The teaching gap: Best ideas from the world's teachers for improving education in the classroom.* New York: The Free Press.

Taggart, G. L., & Wilson, A. P. (1998). *Promoting reflective thinking in teachers: 44 action strategies.* Thousand Oaks, CA: Corwin Press.

Texas Center for Educational Research. (2000). *The cost of teacher turnover.* Austin, TX: Texas State Board of Educator Certification.

Veenman, S. (1984). Perceived problems of beginning teachers. *Review of Educational Research, 54*(2), 143–178.

Villani, S. (2002). *Mentoring new teachers: Models of induction and support.* Thousand Oaks, CA: Corwin Press.

WestEd. (2002). How to support beginning teachers. *R & D Alert, 4*(2). San Francisco: Author.

Wong, H. K. (2004). Induction programs that keep new teachers teaching and improving. *NASSP Bulletin, 88*(638), 41–58.

Wong, H. K., Britton, T., & Ganzer, T. (2005). What the world can teach us about new teacher induction. *Phi Delta Kappan, 86*(5), 379–384.

About the Authors

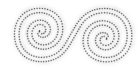

Kathy Dunne

Kathy Dunne, Director of Professional Development for WestEd's Learning Innovations, manages and coordinates large-scale professional development and technical assistance efforts. She has worked with numerous state agencies on policy issues related to the induction and certification of teachers and administrators, and she also provides training, facilitation, and consultation to schools, districts, and institutions of higher education.

A central aspect of her work is providing training for mentors, coaches, and administrators as well as mentor program development support for mentor program planning groups. Much of Dunne's work with mentors and coaches has been in the content areas of mathematics and science. She has served as project director for the NSF-funded Teachers as Learners project, which resulted in the video-based *Teachers as Learners: A Multimedia Kit for Professional Development in Science and Mathematics*.

Dunne is a primary author of *Mentoring: A Resource and Training Guide for Educators; Teachers as Learners: Professional Development in Science and Mathematics: Facilitator's Guide; Mentoring New Teachers Through Collaborative Coaching: Linking Teacher and Student Learning;* and *Mentoring New Teachers Through Collaborative Coaching: Facilitation and Training Guide.*

She has been a high school and middle school classroom teacher, a college instructor, and a curriculum supervisor for a state department of education. She received a B.S. in physical education and an M.Ed. in secondary education from the University of New Hampshire.

Susan Villani

In her joint role as Senior Program Associate and Senior Research Associate for WestEd's Learning Innovations, Susan Villani specializes in designing and facilitating professional development. She works with schools, districts, education collaboratives, and departments of education to tailor program offerings to their specific needs. A particular focus is in the area of mentoring and induction programs for new teachers and new principals. She helps groups design such programs and offers professional development for both mentor teachers and administrators.

Villani has more than 25 years experience as an elementary school teacher and principal, and she was president of the North East Coast Coalition of Educational Leaders, through which she worked with New England educators to promote women and other minorities in education leadership. She was an adjunct faculty member at Lesley University for ten years, specializing in graduate courses on equity and action research. She is the author of *Are You Sure You're the Principal: On Being an Authentic Leader; Mentoring Programs for New Teachers: Models of Induction and Support;* and *Mentoring and Induction Programs That Support New Principals;* in addition to *Mentoring New Teachers Through Collaborative Coaching: Linking Teacher and Student Learning;* and *Mentoring New Teachers Through Collaborative Coaching: Facilitation and Training Guide.*

Villani received a B.A. in business administration from Harpur College, S.U.N.Y. at Binghamton, an M.Ed. in elementary education from Tufts University, and an Ed.D. in educational administration from Northeastern University.

Appendix A
Selected Models of Mentoring and Induction

Program	Student Population	Unique Feature of Program	Duration	Funding	Mentor Responsibilities	Contact Information
Aurora, CO	28,313 in K–12 and some post-secondary	continuum of skills correlated with state standards; district resource teachers support mentors	1 year	district and grants	full-time teachers	Linda Damon, Director of Professional Development 303-340-0859 lindad@hline.aps.k12.co.us
BTSA, Pajaro Valley, CA	19,400 in K–12	full-time release for advisors; statewide program development and implementation	2 years	state and district	full-time mentors	Ellen Moir, Director, New Teacher Center, University of California, Santa Cruz 831-459-4323 moir@cats.ucsc.edu
Dover-Sherborn, MA	1,982 in K–12	teacher leaders coordinate the program and do most of the training	1 year	state grant and local education fund	full-time teachers	Martin Moran, Teacher Leader 508-785-0635 moranm@doversherborn.org
Glendale Union HS, AZ	13,683 in 9–12	3-year program of support for new teachers in regional high school district	3 years	district	part-time teachers	Vernon Jacobs, Associate Superintendent 623-435-6000 x6002 vejacobs@guhsdaz.org
Lee County, NC	8,100 in K–12	taught by classroom teachers, for classroom teachers	3 years	state and local	full-time teachers/full-time mentors	Lou Coggins, Director 919-776-7541 x313 lcoggins.ls@lee.k12.nc.us
Newport News, VA	33,000 in PreK–12	PATHWISE induction model	1 year, possibly 2 years	local and state	full-time teachers	Kathleen Pietrasanta, Staff Development Coordinator 757-591-4584 Kathleen.pietrasanta@nn.k12.va.us
North Haven Public Schools, North Haven, CT	3,486	Program is part of the state's BEST program	2 years, 3 if needed	district and state, which gives districts $200 per new teacher	full-time teachers	Marie Diamond, Director of Curriculum and Instruction 203-239-2581 x327 fax: 203-234-9811 diamond.marie@north-haven.k12.ct.us

87

Program	Student Population	Unique Feature of Program	Duration	Funding	Mentor Responsibilities	Contact Information
Rochester, NY	38,000 in PreK–Adult Ed	peer assistance and review	1 year, possibly longer	district, state, and grants	part-time teachers	Marie Constanza, Mentor Program Director 585-262-8541 Marie.Constanza@rcsdkk12.org
Saint Paul, MN	46,000 in K–12	Learning Circles: small groups of teachers meet monthly with resource colleague to discuss issues of their choosing	3 years	district, grant, and union	full-time teachers	Maria Lamb, Chief Education Officer with the Office of Instructional Services 651-767-8139 maria.lamb@spps.org
STEP Project, MT	159,988 in K–12 (statewide)	telecommunications used for mentoring beginning mathematics, science, and elementary teachers in this large, rural state	2 years, possibly longer	National Science Foundation and state	full-time teachers	Elizabeth Swanson, STEP Project PI 406-994-6768 eswanson@montana.edu
Vicksburg, MI	2,780 in K–12	creative funding of instructional specialists; 3 years of coaching and coursework	3 years	district and creative	full-time teachers/ full-time mentors	Pat Wilson O'Leary, Instructional Specialist 269-321-1038 fax: 269-321-1055 patwo@vicksburg.k12.mi.us

Note. For more information about these programs, see *Mentoring Programs for New Teachers: Models of Induction and Support,* by Susan Villani, 2002, Thousand Oaks, CA: Corwin Press.

Appendix B
Professional Development for Mentors During the School Year

Initial training for mentors should be followed by professional development that continues to support mentors throughout the year. The content of this training will vary depending on the district goals for the program. Representative topics include the following:

- developing a trusting relationship;

- assessing new teachers' needs;

- learning about the cultural identities of the new teachers in the school community and utilizing this knowledge in mentoring them;

- using coaching strategies, including conducting a planning conversation, observing new teachers in their classrooms and gathering data, and scripting a lesson;

- conducting a reflecting conversation, linking new teachers to resources;

- becoming knowledgeable about ways to promote reflection;

- identifying and responding to the diverse needs of students;

- learning about the cultural identities of students in the school community and using this knowledge in lesson planning and interaction with students and their families;

- becoming familiar with community resources to support students and their families and knowing the district and/or state procedures for securing these resources when needed;

- knowing legal issues in education and how they affect teachers' practices;

- understanding and utilizing theories of adult development and the change process as they relate to mentoring;

- becoming familiar with the different instructional leadership behaviors that mentors may use with new teachers, depending on the need for structure and information exhibited by the new teachers in different situations and/or aspects of the curriculum;

- fostering a disposition toward self-reflection and improvement of teaching practices;

- determining appropriate supports and challenges; and

- facilitating independence.

Appendix C
Roles and Responsibilities of Key Shareholders in a Mentor Program
(Hopkinton, MA, Public Schools)

ROLE	AWARENESS	RESPONSIBILITIES
Mentor	• Passionately believe in mentoring as a philosophy • Committed to the personal and professional growth of new teachers • Familiar with the components of the mentor program • Knowledgeable about the program's requirements, such as the training sessions, observations, conferencing, ongoing peer support meetings • Able to foster new teachers' growth, recognizing that the professional growth of new teachers is ultimately the new teachers' responsibility • Understand the importance of trust and confidentiality • Understand the realities and stresses of first-year teachers	• Support new teacher in a confidential, non-evaluative relationship • Promote positive school culture and a problem-solving approach to challenges • Serve as a liaison with other teachers to allow new teachers to use resources and to observe different instruction practices • Reduce isolation of the new teacher by making her/him feel valued as a member of the school community formally and informally • Promote mutual learning with partner • Promote new teacher's awareness of school district policies and practices • Encourage new teacher to voice opinions and/or concerns • Contact new teacher as soon as match is announced • Meet new teacher at summer orientation and participate in sessions • Meet once a week for at least an hour at a regularly scheduled time for first three months, then meet every other week for three months, then meet monthly for the rest of the year • Maintain a log of meetings and topics discussed (for own use only) • Complete end-of-year questionnaire • Do non-evaluative classroom observations and coaching three times per year in addition to informal classroom visits (one observation before November 15, one before January 31, and one before March 30)

ROLE	AWARENESS	RESPONSIBILITIES
Mentor Leaders	• Passionately believe in mentoring as a philosophy • Be committed to the personal and professional growth of new teachers • Be familiar with the components of the mentor program • Be knowledgeable about the program's requirements, such as the training sessions, observations, conferencing, ongoing peer support meetings • Foster new teachers' growth, recognizing that the professional growth of new teachers is ultimately the new teachers' responsibility • Understand the importance of trust and confidentiality • Understand the realities and stresses of first-year teachers and mentors	• Work collaboratively with administrators to promote the district vision and goals • Serve as a liaison with other teachers to allow new teachers to use resources and to observe different instruction practices • Develop or give input on design of new teacher orientations, new teacher support, and continued professional development • Consider issue of how to best match specialists with — or as — mentors • Touch base individually with each mentor and new teacher once a month to check on the functionality of the program • Check with principal periodically regarding administration of the program • Meet monthly with mentor leaders for problem solving and sharing • Promote the working relationships between mentors and new teachers if needed and assist in the decision of a pair to end the partnership • Tell principal if a pairing is ending; the principal will then assign a new mentor and prorate mentor salary for past and present mentors • Help facilitate coverage for non-evaluative classroom observation if needed
New Teachers	• Recognize mentoring as a positive experience and work with the support network that the system has provided • Be knowledgeable about the goals of the program and all of its requirements • Be willing to reflect upon one's ongoing development in teaching • Understand the importance of trust and confidentiality • Acknowledge stresses new teachers may experience	• Be willing to reflect on craft • Participate in the three-day orientation program in August • Observe confidentiality • Participate in three non-evaluative classroom observations and coaching sessions with mentor: one before November 15, the second before January 31, the third before March 30 • Observe mentor at least once by November 15; observe another teacher at least once by March 30 • Meet with mentor one hour per week for first three months, then every other week for the next three months, then once a month for the rest of the year • Maintain a log of meetings and topics discussed (for own use only) • Develop own teaching understandings and methods based on reflective practice • Complete end-of-year questionnaire • Share in the responsibility with mentor for weekly meeting agenda

Appendix C: Roles and Responsibilities of Key Shareholders in a Mentor Program

ROLE	AWARENESS	RESPONSIBILITIES
Principals	• Become knowledgeable about the program and provide input in designing it • Inform the faculty and parents about the program and its benefits • Inform prospective teachers, new teachers, and potential mentors about the details and requirements of the program • Recognize the role of the mentor as the day-to-day and first-line support for new teachers • Understand the importance of trust and confidentiality	• Match new teachers and mentors, with input from mentor leaders when possible • Introduce mentors and new teachers when match is made • Find coverage (in advance) for classroom observations, coaching, and/or classroom visits when needed • Select the mentor leader • Maintain confidentiality • Respect the new teacher/mentor relationship and address conversations about new teacher with new teacher, not with mentor • Convey confidence in and the value of the mentor program • Inform new teachers of the evaluation process • Be involved in the ongoing evaluation of the mentor program
Superintendents and Assistant Superintendents	• Become knowledgeable about the program and attend the summer orientation program • Act as liaison to the community and the school community • Inform the faculty and parents about the program and its benefits • Inform prospective teachers, new teachers, and potential mentors about the details and requirements of the program • Recognize the role of the mentor as the day-to-day and first-line support for new teachers • Understand the importance of trust and confidentiality	• Approve and promote the program • Provide financial support (professional development, grants, etc.) • Facilitate contractual discussions that support the program • Communicate with the administrative team about the need for a mentor program • Promote and implement the program • Understand the systemwide benefits of mentoring • Acknowledge and recognize the contributions of the mentors • Respect confidentiality between mentors and new teachers • Provide time for mentoring to take place • Provide substitutes to allow for observations • Be involved in the ongoing evaluation of the program • Check with administration on progress of the program • Arrange for end-of-year report to school committee [board]
School Committee [Board] Members	• Become knowledgeable about the program and its components	Support • Provide financial support • Facilitate contractual negotiations that support mentoring • Approve the program • Express public support for the program • Participate in the recognition of the mentors Evaluation • Be involved in the ongoing evaluation of the program • Allow time for reports by mentors and new teachers to the school committee [board]

Note. This document is reprinted with permission of Hopkinton (MA) Public Schools.

Appendix D
Ten Ways Principals Can Support New Teachers and Their Mentors

1. Develop and/or support a mentor program in your school or district.

2. Encourage master teachers to become mentors.

3. Make sure that new teachers are not given the most difficult teaching assignments or schedules and do not have too many different class preparations.

4. Support new teachers and mentors with
   - common planning time,
   - release time for observations and conferencing, and
   - remuneration for mentors.

5. Make sure that mentors are matched with partners as soon as possible.

6. Involve the rest of the faculty in understanding the mentor program.

7. Encourage new teachers to focus on teaching the first year or two and forego other responsibilities such as coaching and advising activities.

8. Respect the confidentiality of the mentoring relationship.

9. Anticipate the additional challenges faced by a diverse teaching staff and implement supports.

10. Involve families in supporting new teachers.

Appendix E
Topics and Resources for New Teacher Induction

Some key topics for new teacher induction reflect the range of learning to be addressed — from informational and procedural to conceptual and pedagogical:

- understanding cultural diversity and special needs as they affect student learning;
- classroom management;
- cooperative learning;
- instructional strategies;
- communication skills; and
- use of technology.

The following resources help orient and support the new teacher:

- a history of the district's induction program;
- a description of roles — for example, mentor, new teacher, administrator, other faculty members, faculty from teacher-preparation institutions;
- information on the school district and the teachers' union — for example, the district's philosophy, purpose and members of the school board, personnel flow chart for the district, special services available in the district, a list of curriculum guides, an organization structure for the teachers' union, the contract between the teachers' union and the district, district committees, the credit union, discipline policies;
- recertification/relicensing procedures and contact people;
- a list of resources — for example, state education agency, teacher centers, libraries, local colleges and universities, and conferences — with accompanying contact persons, addresses, and telephone numbers;
- school and mentor program handbooks; and
- a checklist for preparing for the first day of school.

Also available from WestEd

Kathy Dunne and Susan Villani
$149.95 / 300 pages / binder + CD
ISBN: 978-0-914409-31-1
www.WestEd.org/cs/we/view/rs/813

For information about the workshops,
customized training, or technical
assistance, contact WestEd:

Mark Kerr at 415.615.3219
mkerr@WestEd.org

or Kathy Dunne at 781.481.1100
kdunne@WestEd.org

Mentoring New Teachers Through Collaborative Coaching:
Facilitation and Training Guide

Designed for professional developers who work with mentors, this
Facilitation and Training Guide can be used to recreate or customize
the comprehensive mentoring program developed by WestEd's Kathy
Dunne and Susan Villani and used with schools and districts across the
country. The 39 step-by-step activities included in the binder make it
possible to pick and choose those that best fit local needs. In addition,
sample agendas for three-day and five-day workshops represent field-
tested workshops that have been used successfully in many different
contexts. Each activity is complete with process steps, facilitator notes
and hints, and all necessary handouts, overheads, and PowerPoint slides.
In addition to the binder materials, a CD provides convenient storage for
electronic versions of the handouts, overheads, slides, and agendas.

Professional Development for Mentoring New Teachers Through
Collaborative Coaching

Using the principles and approaches described in *Mentoring New
Teachers Through Collaborative Coaching: Linking Teacher and
Student Learning*, and drawing on the tools and activities in the
companion *Facilitation and Training Guide*, WestEd now offers
customized mentoring professional development programs for
schools, districts, and states in four focus areas:

>> Essential Skills for Mentoring New Teachers

>> Lead Mentor Training: Enhancing Teacher Leadership to Mentor
and Coach

>> The Administrator's Role in Mentoring and Coaching New Teachers

>> Mentoring Professional Development Design Course

In the core workshop, Essential Skills for Mentoring New Teachers,
mentor teachers and other participants clarify the qualities and roles of
effective mentor teachers, understand the needs of new teachers and how
to respond as those needs shift, and develop the skills and understanding
to serve as a new teacher's collaborative coach. Research has found that
such mentoring approaches, while improving new teachers' content
knowledge and pedagogy, have the corollary effect of reducing class
management problems. Likewise, it has long been recognized that
effective mentoring programs increase new teachers' professional
satisfaction and reduce the rate of new teacher attrition.

Also available from WestEd

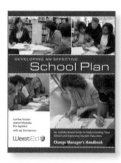

LoriVan Houten, Jeanne Miyasaka,
and Kim Agullard with Joy Zimmerman

$129.95 / 273 pages /
two trade paper books + CD

ISBN: 978-0-914409-26-7

www.WestEd.org/cs/we/view/rs/795

Developing an Effective School Plan: An Activity-Based Guide to Understanding Your School and Improving Student Outcomes

School improvement plans have the potential to focus schools on high-need and high-leverage objectives. By better understanding how to develop, implement, and monitor an improvement plan, schools can close achievement gaps and enhance learning for all of their students. Over the years, WestEd staff have been called on by literally hundreds of schools to help them improve. This school improvement package — facilitation guide, activities, interactive tools, and CD — represents the distillation and thoughtful organization of what WestEd staff have learned firsthand from their work with diverse schools across the country. Recognizing that all schools start the improvement process with different needs and degrees of capacity, the materials are very flexible — approachable, yet structured for deep investigations as needed.

WestEd

$15.95 / 57 pages / trade paper

ISBN: 978-0-914409-17-5

www.WestEd.org/cs/we/view/rs/688

Moving Leadership Standards Into Everyday Work: Descriptions of Practice

The descriptions of practice (DOPs) introduced here were developed to enhance the usefulness of research-based leadership standards, including the widely used California Professional Standards for Education Leaders (CPSELs) and the nationally developed Interstate School Leaders Licensure Consortium (ISLLC) standards. For each of six broad standards, the DOPs identify the underlying goals and provide a detailed narrative describing specific administrator actions, attitudes, and understanding needed to attain each goal. Key aspects of what each standard looks like in action are also described across a four-level continuum of developing practice. Coupled with the standards, the DOPs can serve as a (1) starting point for developing credentialing criteria, (2) guide for planning leadership preparation or professional development, (3) basis for clarifying performance expectations, and (4) mirror for an administrator's self-reflection and professional goal-setting.

To find information on WestEd research and services, or to sign up for our monthly *E-Bulletin* newsletter and other free reports, visit www.WestEd.org. To order call toll-free at 888 C-WESTED [888.293.7833]. To order online, visit www.WestEd.org/products.